THE PRINCIPAL AS A LEARNING-LEADER

Motivating Students by Emphasizing Achievement

M. Scott Norton and Larry K. Kelly

Rowman & Littlefield Education

A Division of
ROWMAN & LITTLEFIELD PUBLISHERS, INC.
Lanham • New York • Toronto • Plymouth, UK

Published by Rowman & Littlefield Education
A division of Rowman & Littlefield Publishers, Inc.
A wholly owned subsidiary of The Rowman & Littlefield Publishing Group, Inc.
4501 Forbes Boulevard, Suite 200, Lanham, Maryland 20706
www.rowman.com

10 Thornbury Road, Plymouth PL6 7PP, United Kingdom

Copyright © 2013 by M. Scott Norton and Larry K. Kelly

All rights reserved. No part of this book may be reproduced in any form or by any electronic or mechanical means, including information storage and retrieval systems, without written permission from the publisher, except by a reviewer who may quote passages in a review.

British Library Cataloguing in Publication Information Available

Library of Congress Cataloging-in-Publication Data

Norton, M. Scott.
  The principal as a learning-leader : motivating students by emphasizing achievement / M. Scott Norton and Larry K. Kelly.
    p. cm.
  Includes bibliographical references.
  ISBN 978-1-61048-806-8 (cloth)—ISBN 978-1-61048-807-5 (pbk.)—
ISBN 978-1-61048-808-2 (electronic)
  1. School principals—Rating of. 2. Academic achievement. I. Kelly, Larry K., 1936- II. Title.
  LB2831.96.N67 2013
  371.26—dc23
                                                            2012030849

CONTENTS

Preface v

Introduction vii

1   Establishing a Foundation for the Implementation of Successful Learning Experiences for All Students   1

2   Preparing, Organizing, and Enabling the Faculty and Staff for a Learning-Centered School   31

3   The Development of a School Climate and Culture Learning-Leadership: Creating the Atmosphere for a Learning Environment   61

4   Roles and Responsibilities for Establishing a Positive Learning Environment   95

5   The Principal: A Learning-Leader at Work   123

About the Authors   161

Preface

This book is intended for the school leader that currently is serving as a practitioner in the field. Thus, the book focuses on those individuals in the school who are serving in a leadership role and have faced many of the contemporary problems relative to such matters as underperforming schools, student dropout rates, low student achievement, and student performance accountability. However, those school leaders that are experiencing success in creating a learning culture in their school also will find the book to be beneficial for their continued professional growth. In addition, those individuals who aspire to a career in the principalship will find the information in the book of special value. School boards are making new demands for student learning that commonly are interpreted as "student failure is no option, or else!"

In most instances, the professional preparation of the principal includes managerial responsibilities related to budgeting, facility planning, personnel administration, and other aspects of organizing and managing the school's operations.

Such preparation might not include sufficient preparation in the areas of student learning, curriculum development, and academic performance assessments. Today, the primary need for school leadership centers on the fostering of student achievement and establishing a learning culture in the school.

The primary purpose of the book is to provide practicing school principals and others who aspire to that role to be able to meet the challenges related to learning leadership. The book serves as a guide for ensuring the accomplishment of the goal of establishing a learning culture in the school. Persons who use the book will gain the knowledge and skills useful in becoming an effective learning-leader. Each chapter presents creative but practical suggestions for achieving that objective.

PREFACE

The book will help the principal answer the following questions: Are you truly a learning-leader? Are your students enrolled in a school with a learning culture? In what ways does your personal behavior demonstrate the traits of an effective learning-leader? Am I doing what truly is in the best interests of each individual student regarding his or her learning achievement? Do I have an organized procedure for assessing student achievement and using data results to change students' programs accordingly? Am I able to provide credible evidence that our program of offerings and activities is resulting in continuous student growth?

When you think about or are asked about your personal administrative strengths, does your answer reflect those of a learning-leader? An opportunity for you to assess your learning-leadership is provided at the outset of the book. You can participate in activities being discussed in the chapters and test the many recommendations for improving student learning along the way.

The book's special features include the fact that the book is reader friendly. It provides a clear definition of learning-leadership and how it varies from the definition of an instructional leader. The focus on program practices that are in the best interests of students and support successful learning results is present throughout the book. Snapshots of effective practices, as reported by successful learning-leaders, are presented in each chapter. Engaging and reengaging students in the learning process are considered one of the book's special features. The book presents several models for the school principal to consider for establishing a learning culture in the school and school community.

The importance of accountability, partnerships, and collaboratives is considered in-depth. Strategies for demonstrating accountability, the special needs of a successful school partnership, and models for implementing these important program provisions are given special attention.

The importance of establishing a healthy climate, as it relates to the improvement of student achievement in the school, is given primary consideration. We submit that one of the key factors for realizing improvements in student achievement is that of establishing positive relationships among teachers, students, administrators, and stakeholders in the school community.

Tools and techniques are provided that enable the school principal to foster a learning climate that engages all students, teachers, staff personnel, parents, and others in the learning process. How successful principal learning-leaders work to foster a learning-centered culture in the school is emphasized throughout the book.

Introduction

School leaders today are pressed to provide evidence of continuous student success relative to academic achievement. Effective schools are judged primarily by student academic test results in the key subject areas of mathematics, science, reading, and English studies. The school's quality rating no longer is based primarily on such provisions as the school's comprehensive curriculum provisions, teacher performance measures, or student behavioral data. Rather, student academic results as measured by federal, state, and local standards commonly determine the fate of the school, the school leaders, and the school's teachers.

It isn't that a good school public relations program, winning sports program, or student retention rate is not important, it is just that these factors tend to fade into the background when the academic achievement data results fall below the achievement benchmarks expected of student learners. When the question is asked, "What is the primary role of the school principal," answers such as to plan and organize the school's program, to develop a program of effective public relations, or to provide professional growth opportunities for the faculty and staff fall short of today's accountability demands. Without question, the school principal's major role is to serve as the learning-leader of the school and to develop a learning culture within the school community.

This book has been written primarily for the practicing school principal and other individuals who aspire to this leadership position. We take a close look at the best practices of individuals that have been identified as learning-leaders. How do these leaders work to plan and implement a learning-centered environment in the school? We report basic research that supports best practices for ensuring positive student achievement.

INTRODUCTION

We examine and report on empirical practices that can serve as a guide for implementing successful student achievement strategies in the school.

We achieve the foregoing objectives by bringing the reader into the discussions in each chapter of the book. For example, we challenge the reader to participate in several exercises during the reading of each chapter. As school principal, you will be asked to take the LLTA (Learning-Leader's Traits Assessment) at the outset of chapter 1. The responses of the reader provide a rating level for the individual as related to his/her status as a learning-leader.

The chapter then provides the rationale for each question posed in the LLTA and serves as a learning base for the remainder of the chapter. The reader is asked to take a moment to consider a relevant case study or to review a snapshot in relation to their school's current status of practice.

Snapshots relating to the work of learning-leaders in the field, opportunities for the reader to stop and think about a concept being discussed in relation to his/her own practices, models of best practice that can be implemented in the principal's present school situation, and other application exercises that bring the reader into the ongoing discussion are in evidence in each chapter of the book.

The book is organized within five chapters. Chapter 1 establishes the foundation for the implementation of successful learning experiences for all students. The building of a learning culture in the school and the traits and behaviors of a learning-leader are set forth. Competency-based performance as related to learning-leadership is discussed. Information concerning how to set standards for student achievement and how such standards can serve toward the building of a learning-centered school are detailed. Each chapter includes application exercises that serve to extend the reader's knowledge and skills.

In chapter 2 the preparing, equipping, and enabling of the faculty and staff for a learning-centered school are detailed. The special skills of organization for student learning loom important in this chapter. The important strategies of challenging and motivating the faculty toward becoming a learning-centered school are emphasized. New terms that the reader likely will encounter include *stretch goals*, *results-oriented teaching and learning*, *strategic partnerships*, *zest factors*, and others that focus on student achievement.

How does school climate and culture influence student achievement? What does the research say? Chapter 3 discusses the paramount importance of these concepts in detail. Similarities between school climate and school culture are clarified in this chapter, and ways to improve school climate are presented in-depth.

The importance of a healthy school environment for fostering student achievement is considered further in chapter 4. What does it mean to create a school-community culture that fosters student learning? How does the school principal foster teacher learning-leadership in the school? These important questions are answered in this chapter.

Best practices of successful learning-leaders are identified. Challenges facing school principals in the area of accountability are detailed. How does the principal provide stu-

INTRODUCTION

dent achievement evidence that really counts? Why leaders and faculty personnel need to give special attention to student learning styles is developed in this chapter.

A unique and challenging topic considered in chapter 4 is how to plan, organize, and implement effective programs of collaboration and partnerships for the purpose of promoting student learning. We submit that comprehensive collaboration and the establishment of meaningful partnerships within the school community will be a significant future development for fostering a learning school community.

We endeavor to help school leaders gain a better understanding of their own personal status regarding learning-leadership by providing the knowledge, tools, and techniques for building a learning culture in the school. Implicit in this effort is a "challenge" to examine one's current beliefs, values, and traits relative to the most effective practices implemented by successful learning-leaders. We believe that the information provided in this book will result in renewed motivation for the reader to become increasingly effective in serving as a true learning-leader for the purpose of helping all students be more successful as learners.

1

Establishing a Foundation for the Implementation of Successful Learning Experiences for All Students

THE STORY OF MARIA

Maria was a fifth-grade student who had performed academically at grade level in grades 1 through 4. During the first year of grade 5, however, her performances in all subjects began to decline. Her perfect attendance record ended and she withdrew participation in two after-school activities. When her teacher, Miss Jenkins, asked her about her withdrawal from these activities, she said, "I just lost interest."

The one out-of-school activity that Maria did continue was her dancing lessons. Although the teacher didn't think much about it at first, Maria's classroom work seemed to pick up somewhat on Fridays. This just happened to be the day after Maria's after-school dancing lessons.

Miss Jenkins decided to call Maria's parents. She indicated that she was concerned about Maria's apparent disengagement in classroom and out-of-class activities. Maria's mother simply stated that her daughter's behavior was similar at home. That perhaps it was just a temporary thing relative to children growing up.

Miss Jenkins wasn't satisfied with the parent's response and decided to consult with the school principal on this matter. The school principal, Mr. Mehuron, made a follow-up call to Maria's parents. At one point he suggested that Maria have a physical examination by the family doctor. The school nurse did confer with Maria but found no apparent medical reasons for her current behavior. However, she did learn that Maria's eating habits needed some attention. Arrangements were made with the cafeteria manager for Maria to have a nourishing breakfast each morning and noon at school.

CHAPTER 1

A call was made to Maria's dancing instructor. The dancing instructor reported that Maria's attitude and energy in her classes were quite good; she often stayed after class to practice her dancing lessons. In fact, Maria was one of the instructor's most enthusiastic students.

This was enough information for Miss Jenkins to ask Maria to remain a few minutes after school. The teacher had borrowed several books from the dancing studio, and the public librarian suggested other books on dancing that Maria might enjoy. When she met with Maria, the teacher encouraged her to select three or four books on various dancing topics. She also gained approval from the school principal to subscribe to one of the journals on dance around the world.

Miss Jenkins used Maria's interest in dancing to continue her classroom learning. She reviewed Maria's recent homework assignments and test scores on latest achievement tests. The teacher used the same classroom objectives and grade standards in assigning Marie reading lessons on topics such as the history of dance. Her lessons in spelling and grammar, reading, writing, music, and art focused on dance. On one occasion, Maria completed an essay on the topic of mathematics and the fine arts.

With the help of Miss Jenkins, the school's music teacher, and the school principal, Maria helped in the planning of a special school talent show. Miss Jenkins motivated Maria's reengagement in learning by capitalizing on her personal strengths and interests. Now in grade 7 and in a middle school, Maria is successfully progressing in her academic subjects and continues to expand her interests in other extracurricular subjects.

No one can say what Maria's fate might have been if a teacher and the school principal had not acted in her behalf. But if she had continued to decline academically, her fate might have been to drop out of school. Thanks to a teacher learning-leader and a supportive school principal, Maria was reengaged in learning in a student-centered environment. Fortunately, Maria was enrolled in a school with a community learning culture. Many individuals in the school and in the community contributed to Maria's reengagement in learning.

Perhaps you have been part of a similar instance when a student's academic achievement needed your personal support. As a school principal, you presently have students with such special needs. We submit that all of your students need and deserve your personal attention and support.

WHAT THIS BOOK IS ABOUT

This book is about you and your status as a learning-leader. One of our purposes is illustrated by the foregoing story. Consider a few of the words included in the story of Maria. Learning culture, reengagement, personal strengths and interests, academic achievement, personal support, classroom objectives, learning-leader, grade standards, and student-centered environment are among the words in Marie's story. Each word commonly is a part of a learning-leader's vocabulary. A learning-leader focuses on student learning; learning results serve as his or her tests of accountability.

We have never encountered a teacher that didn't want to become a better teacher. We believe the same about school principals. We believe that you want to improve your personal performance. However, we want you to ask yourself several questions: Are you truly a learning-leader? Are your students enrolled in a school with a learning culture? In what ways does your personal behavior demonstrate the traits of a true learning-leader? When you think about or are asked about your personal administrative strengths, does your answer reflect those of a learning-leader? Are you willing to find out?

We hope that you will take the following Learning-Leader's Traits Assessment (LLTA). In order for you to determine your LLTA status accurately, you will have to answer the true-or-false and other multiple-choice responses according to your personal and professional beliefs. Only you will see the test results, so don't answer according to what your supervisor might want to hear or what might look good in an interview response. Respond to each entry from your personal perspective.

ASSESSMENT OF YOUR LEARNING-LEADER'S PERSONAL TRAITS

Directions: Check each response that best represents your personal position. Respond according to your beliefs rather than what others might want you to do or what your current school rules might require you to do. The results of the LLTA depend on what you believe, your personal behaviors. Several assessment questions might list several positive responses. You need to select the one that comes closest to your own perspective. If you do not know the correct answer, avoid guessing. Rather than merely guessing, just leave the statement unanswered.

A. True or False

_____1. There is firm evidence that formative classroom assessment is an essential component of classroom work and its development can raise standards of achievement.

_____2. It is the teacher who should be given the sole responsibility for determining how his or her time is used, what is to be monitored, how in-service time and resources are used, and what student assessments should be ongoing.

_____3. The terms *instructional leadership* and *learning-leader* are synonymous and thus have the same primary educational focus.

_____4. Monitoring staff on their collection and use of data is a critical way to keep staff clear about your (the principal's) priorities.

_____5. Although school climate does reflect the social and interpersonal status of administrator, staff, and student relationships in the school, research evidence

CHAPTER 1

has not found that student achievement is improved when the school's climate is improved.

_____6. High-performing schools place an emphasis on accountability.

_____7. Recent research findings reveal that giving primary attention to student learning results is faulty. Rather, primary attention should be given to improving the marginal teacher's performance.

_____8. Determining the most essential needs of the school's program offerings is best determined by a consensus of the parents of the children in the school.

_____9. Best student learning will result when the school has adopted a school mission.

_____10. When all is said and done, having each teacher do his or her thing regarding the determination of classroom goals and deciding what to teach and how to teach it is best for student learning.

B. Multiple Choice and Completion Questions

Directions: Choose the response that is closest to *your* own personal disposition—the one that best represents your personal behavior or the one that you most likely would pursue. The validity of the assessment depends largely on whether or not your response reflects you as an individual—your personal thinking and behavior. Don't be concerned that the item is outside your administrative role. It is your belief about the matter that's important.

1. Which statement on your school marquee would bring you the most personal satisfaction?
    a. School's Football Team Wins State Championship
    b. School's Science Teacher, Sharon Lloyd, Named Teacher of the Year by State Teachers' Association
    c. School's Principal, (Your Name), Named Principal of the Year by the State Administrators' Association
    d. Senior Student, Gwen Ryon, Wins First Prize at Regional Student Editorial Writing Conference

2. Check the agenda for your most recent faculty meeting. List three of the topics discussed at that meeting:
    _____
    _____
    _____

3. Which statement below is one of the *truest tests* of what one believes is really important in your school organization?
    a. The allocation of time devoted to an issue on both the annual calendar and within the daily schedule
    b. How parents perceive the quality of the school program
    c. The informal staff get-togethers for purposes of socialization
    d. The time spent on deciding on a school mission statement

4. The following statements are those of school principals in response to the question "Why did you decide to become a school principal?" Which one is most similar to the reason that you entered the role?
    a. I enjoyed various leadership roles during my high school years and then served as president of the Students' Association while attending college. I always enjoyed serving in a leadership position and helping to decide on student policies. This led me into school administration.
    b. I knew a family whose father was a school principal. He seemed to enjoy the role as principal and was able to provide well for his family. I always wanted to do the best to provide for my family. This motivated me to go into education and ultimately the school principalship.
    c. Actually, my career as a principal was somewhat by chance. I wasn't sure about my major during the first two years of college and then I enrolled in two education classes. This led to a degree in teaching and later experience as a department chair. When an assistant principal's position opened in the district, I applied and was selected for that role. I guess the rest is history.
    d. None of the above is similar to the reason that I entered the role of school principal. I entered the role of principal because: _____ _____.

5. The six-month student achievement scores for each elementary school class were collected and discussed. The large majority of the teachers' classes showed achievement progress. However, three classes showed no progress with one class showing a slight regression. Which entry below reflects your personal opinion as a logical conclusion about this matter?
    a. The results simply reflect what happens according to the normal curve of learning.
    b. The principal probably did not explain the test results clearly to the teachers.
    c. The regressions likely were due to the fact that these teachers did not fully understand what the data said and how to use the data.
    d. There is no way for the school principal to know what happened in the classes where no progress was realized.

6. As the leader for student learning, the school principal guides teachers in several ways. Which entry below is the behavior that most likely would be least effective in helping the teacher improve student learning results?
    a. Discuss the school's vision and how the teacher can communicate high expectations for all students
    b. Provide collegial and honest feedback on teaching and learning results
    c. Translate state and school standards to a scope and sequence curriculum
    d. Write a note for the record that details the teacher's instructional weaknesses and give the note to him or her for personal reflection

CHAPTER 1

7. The members of the learning team for middle school student Tyler Scott are meeting to examine data concerning his learning progress and determine an initial learning plan for the second semester. Emphasis will be given to the required and elective courses that Tyler will take, including his participation in extracurricular activities. Tyler has been achieving slightly below grade level in all of his first-semester courses, except music appreciation.

    Persons on the learning team include the school principal, four of Tyler's first-semester tenth-grade teachers, the school's student counselor, and Tyler's parents. If one additional person could be added to the team, which person below would you select?
    a. The school nurse
    b. The coordinator of extracurricular activities for the school
    c. An unbiased third-party member
    d. Tyler Scott himself
    e. Tyler's first-semester music teacher

8. We often speak of the importance of considering the student's personal needs and interests when making decisions regarding program offerings and activities. In your opinion, how should the student's personal interests and needs best be determined?
    a. These personal needs and interests are best determined by the school district's and state's academic standards for the various grade levels in the school.
    b. These personal needs and interests are best determined by the teachers in the school who know Tyler's achievement record.
    c. These personal needs and interests are best determined by the parents of Tyler Scott.
    d. These personal needs and interests are best determined by the school principal.
    e. These personal needs and interests are best determined by the student himself or herself.

9. Write your personal definition (two or three sentences) of the term *A Learning Culture*.
    a. My definition of the term *A Learning Culture* follows: _____
    _____
    _____
    _____.

10. A teacher in your school says to you, "I just can't teach effectively with special education kids in the room with others who are making great strides in their learning achievement. It just isn't fair to the normal students in the class that I have to spend so much time with the special needs students." Which response below is closest to your response to the teacher?

a. "I understand completely. But we have to include special needs students in all of our regular classrooms by federal law."
b. "I sympathize with your feelings on this matter. Special needs students do require much of a teacher's classroom time. I will try to get some part-time help for you to handle the extra work."
c. "Even if Section 504 of the Rehabilitation Act of 1973 did not prohibit the denial of participation in public education or enjoyment of the benefits of public school programs because of a child's disability, I fully support the concept of an inclusive school whereby each and every child can participate in the normal classroom programs and school activities. Yes, we all will have to make changes in our administration and teaching practices so that all students can contribute to the accomplishment of our school's mission."
d. "Rejection of one of your special needs students to participate fully in all learning activities provided in the classroom would be considered unjust under Section 504 of the Rehabilitation Act of 1973. You and I cannot afford to have legal action taken against the school in this regard. Let's meet with the special education coordinator to see if she has suggestions for working with special needs students in the regular classroom."

11. Your third-grade teacher drops by your office. He tells you that one of his students is doing grade level work in all subject areas but math. He says, "The student is having difficulty moving with the class in math because she hasn't mastered the multiplication tables. I have drilled and drilled her on the tables. I have given extra homework on the tables. I have asked the parents to work with her on the tables. None of these efforts seem to have helped. She can't do multiplication problems, and so I can't move ahead with division. She's holding up other members of the class. I don't see how she can be promoted to fourth grade. She has to know the tables before moving on to more advanced work." Which response below is closest to your advice for the teacher?
    a. Math is always one of those stumbling blocks for some students. You've certainly given this matter your best shot.
    b. What explanation of the multiplication process have you tried? For example, have you shown the student how multiplication ties closely to addition? Such as 4 x 4 is the same as 4 + 4 + 4 + 4?
    c. Learning is not always sequential and linear. Rather than viewing learning as only a building-block procedure, cognitive psychology likens learning more to the building of Tinkertoys. Information is collected and stored in various ways. As new information is gained, some new connections between and among the parts are completed. Over a period of time and as other knowledge is added, it serves to make important connections, and insight results in learning achievement.

d. Well, it's important that you keep on working to improve this student's proficiency in math. Our school's proficiency rating depends quite heavily on the state test results.

12. What is the major difference between the terms *instructional leader* and *learning-leader*?
    a. There is no major difference between the two terms.
    b. One term focuses on instruction and the other on learning.
    c. One term focuses on the improvement of teaching performance and the other on student achievement results.
    d. One term specifies the administrator as the leader and the other term the teacher as the leader.

13. A colleague principal and personal friend of yours comments as follows: "I was well prepared in college for administrative work and have served sixteen years in school administration and the principalship. This new push by the central office personnel to create a learning culture in all the schools in the district doesn't really concern me much. If I am not prepared for such changes now, I never will be." Which response below do you believe is most appropriate?
    a. No need to respond; let friends be friends. I agree, someone is always shuffling the furniture and arguing that change is needed.
    b. This pressure to have a learning culture in the school is just another fad; it will pass just like all the others.
    c. You want to keep your job, don't you? Just go along.
    d. Just think what our schools are all about; student learning is our primary purpose. As school principals, we must learn how to create an environment that supports a learning culture. The schools of yesterday are not the kind that we need for tomorrow.

14. Which one of the following areas of knowledge do you believe is most important in the leadership role?
    a. A deep understanding of how humans learn
    b. The policies and regulations of the school district regarding student discipline
    c. Knowledge and skills of supervision
    d. General knowledge of each subject area taught in the school

15. You are a finalist for the position of principal of a new middle school in your school district. The opening question posed by the president of the school board was as follows: Just why are you applying for the principal's position at our new middle school? Write your primary reason for applying for the position: _____
_____
_____.

16. In your opinion, which entry below is the top priority of the school principal?
    a. Managing the budget and providing adequate teaching resources
    b. Evaluating teacher performance
    c. Fostering appropriate school and parent relationships
    d. Providing leadership for student learning
17. Which one of the three leadership entries below do you consider most important for the school principal? (Note: Each is important, but choose the one that you consider as being most important overall.)
    a. Learning-leadership that focuses on the end results of student achievement and a learning culture in the school-community
    b. Mission leadership that demonstrates the school's primary purpose for its existence
    c. School-community leadership that establishes the fact that the school plays a significant role in the community's life quality
18. Four potential commitments for improving today's school principalship are listed below. All are important considerations. However, choose the one commitment that you believe to be most important for improving the role of the school principal today.
    a. Increase the salaries and fringe benefits for school principals in order to attract and retain quality personnel in the role
    b. Enhance the autonomy and authority of school principals relative to the decision-making process
    c. Alleviate the many stresses of the principal's role by reinventing the principal's role and providing additional administrative help and support
    d. Improve the preparation practices for entering the principalship and focus on instruction and appropriate practice for gaining knowledge, skills, and strategies for improving student learning
19. You are being interviewed for the position of school principal in the largest middle school in the College View School District. You are the present school principal of Roosevelt Elementary School with an enrollment of 500 students. College View has 1,000 students. One interviewer states, "School principals today must assume responsibility for numerous outcomes. How would you demonstrate your accountability as the principal of the College View middle school? Write your brief response here. _____
    _____
    _____
    _____.
20. Which definition below best defines the term *school culture*?
    a. School culture is the set of important assumptions, beliefs, values, and attitudes that members of a school and school system share.

b. School culture is the collective personality of a school and school system. It is the atmosphere as characterized by the social and professional interactions within it.
c. School culture is the way we do things around here.
d. Culture is the ethnic mix of people in the school and school system.

LLTA Answers and Scoring Instructions
The answers for the true-and-false section are 1 T, 2 F, 3 F, 4 T, 5 F, 6 T, 7 F, 8 F, 9 F, 10 F. Answers to the multiple-choice section are 1d; 2, credit if learning is mentioned; 3a; 4d, credit if learning is mentioned; 5c; 6d; 7d; 8e; 9, credit if learning is mentioned; 10c; 11c; 12c; 13d; 14a; 15 (see the answer on page 16); 16a; 17a; 18d; 19, credit if learning is mentioned; 20a. Total the number of correct responses for each section. Multiply this total by 3.3. This is your LLTA score. Example: 8 correct in the true-and-false section and 14 correct in the multiple-choice section = 22 correct x 3.3 = 72.6. The score places you at the "Utilizing" level as shown in figure 1.1.

Now Let's Consider the Answers to the LLTA Exercise
Let's take some time to examine the preferred responses to the LLTA activity. The rationale related to the answers that come closest to those principals who are actually practicing the behaviors of true learning-leaders are discussed. Keep in mind that other responses could be viewed as positive and productive, but not necessarily those of learning-leaders.

True and False Statements
#1—Statement #1 is true. School Improvement in Maryland (2011), in its article *Monitoring Student Progress,* emphasizes that both research and practice support the contention that the monitoring of student performance is needed on an ongoing basis. Black and Wilian (1998) note that assessment evidence is an essential part of classroom work. Its development can raise standards of achievement. The ongoing assessment of student progress along with the assumption of accountability for achievement results are two primary traits of an effective learning-leader.
#2—Statement #2 is false. Your view of the answer to Question #2 might differ. Our view, however, is that teaching no longer is a single's act. Setting school achievement goals, determining growth benchmarks, and implementing coordinated student interventions necessitates team collaboration. The school principal must control learning factors such as time on task and the alignment of instruction to the specific goals and standards set forth by the school's and state's standards. Certainly, the teacher and others play a role in deciding how time is used and what is to be monitored. However, the principal is the learning-leader of the school. As stated by DuFour (2002), "A school's teacher cannot make student learning their focus until they know what each student needs to learn" (p. 12). In a learning culture, decisions

LLTA Score	LLTA Level	Level Defined and Evidence
100–90	Leading	You show comprehensive evidence of having a high level of the behaviors and traits of a practicing learning-leader. Your knowledge level indicates that you have the ability to teach others about its importance for successful student achievement.
89–80	Practicing	You show very good evidence of understanding the behaviors and traits of a learning-leader and can use these skills to improve student learning in everyday practice.
79–70	Utilizing	Your substantial understanding of the concept of a learning-leader allows you to utilize it in several ways in fostering a learning culture in your school.
69–60	Progressing	You reveal a level of knowledge and skills relative to learning leadership that will enable you to make continuous improvement. Keep making an effort to apply the learning-leader behaviors and traits in your everyday administrative practice.
59–50	Initiating	You show some evidence of having the behaviors and traits of a learning-leader. Your ability to use additional traits of learning-leaders will improve by the time you complete your reading/study of this book.
49–Below	Introductory	Your limited knowledge and traits of learning-leadership are inhibiting your success in developing a learning culture in your school. Nevertheless, keep trying. Complete the reading of this book and implement some of the ideas that you found most fascinating. You'll be patting yourself on the back soon if you do.

Figure 1.1. Learning-Leader's Traits Assessment (LLTA) Ratings

CHAPTER 1

on what is taught and how learning is monitored is a team consideration with the school principal serving as the learning-leader.

#3—Statement #3 is false. Instructional leaders focus on individual teachers and their instructional strategies. Learning-leaders focus on student learning results. Instructional leaders emphasize inputs of the learning process; learning-leaders focus on outputs. In brief, learning-leaders place student learning at the center of their decision-making process. The learning-leader keeps the school staff focused on improving student achievement. The two terms, of course, are tied in some respects, but learning-leaders do whatever it takes to improve student achievement.

#4—Statement #4 is true. The saying that "what gets monitored, gets done" applies to the principal's monitoring practices relative to student learning results. As noted in the article *Keep the Focus on Student Achievement,* "When a school devotes considerable time and effort to the continual assessment of a particular condition of outcome, it notifies all members that the condition or outcome is considered important" (Maryland State Department of Education, 2011, p. 1).

#5—Statement #5 is false. The level of health of the school climate weighs heavily on the quality of student achievement. "In fact, the quality of the climate appears to be the single most predictive factor in any school's capacity to promote student achievement" (Shindler, Jones, Williams, Taylor, & Cardenas, p. 1). School climate and student achievement are discussed in detail in chapter 3.

#6—Statement #6 is true. School leaders in learning cultures hold themselves accountable for making certain that all students progress relative to proficient achievement levels and closing the achievement gap for each individual learner.

Empirical evidence supports the belief that learning-leaders and staff personnel want to be held accountable for those results for which they are responsible. They do not want to be held accountable for results that are beyond their jurisdiction or control. This is why the response to Statement #2 above looms important.

The principal, as learning-leader, must help the teaching staff understand the school's and/or state's achievement targets. The principal must work to keep the entire school staff and school-community focused on student achievement goals as the primary work of the school. Growth models that track the achievement progress from one year to the next have proven useful in determining the status of a student's achievement.

#7—Statement #7 is false. On the contrary, attention to student achievement results as opposed to placing emphasis on improving teaching performance has been shown to be more productive. While a school with a learning culture would not dismiss the need to improve teaching performance, this emphasis has not proven to result in sufficient student achievement.

The assumption that in-service efforts, teacher assessment, and other instructional efforts spill over to improved student achievement has not been substantiated. Rather, other factors such as the improvement of school climate and placing emphasis on the principal functioning as a learning-leader hold more promise for improved student achievement.

#8—Statement #8 is false. The learning-leader who has gathered data from various achievement tests, has counseled with teachers, conferred with school counselors, communicated with parents, and paid attention to individual student needs and interests is in the best position to determine student program and activity pursuits. Nevertheless, learning necessitates a team effort in an environment that facilitates the advancement of student and staff learning.

#9—Statement #9 is false. We do not set aside the paramount importance of establishing a viable school mission. However, merely adopting a school mission falls short of what is needed. A viable mission statement cannot be written and adopted overnight. First, the learning-leader, school faculty and staff, parent representatives, and participants from the school-community must deal with the "purpose" questions. Questions such as "Why does our school exist?" or "What is our purpose?" or "What is our reason for being here?" must be deliberately addressed (Norton, Kelly, & Battle, 2012, p. 30).

As suggested by Norton and others (2012), there is a subtle difference between mission and purpose. "Student reasons" underscore the purpose of schools; they exist for their students. The mission statement provides direction for the school based on a perception of the environment. It influences the major direction of a school system. One system may state its primary mission as college preparation, whereas others might concentrate on basic skills, special education, or vocational education (Norton, 2008).

We contend that the best learning takes place when the purpose of the school focuses on student learning and achievement results. The school mission should focus on providing the best learning opportunities so that each and every student learns at his or her success level and achieves at his or her full potential. Furthermore, we take a strong stand against student retention in grade. The volumes of literature on the subject of student retention make it clear that holding a student in-grade for an additional year does not improve student performance or improve other affective behaviors such as social skills, discipline, and self-esteem. "In the final analysis, the student promotion problem will best be resolved when each school's mission becomes that of improving learning for all students, where the focus is on student learning, when failure is not an option, and when each school is led by a learning-centered principal with learning-leaders teaching in every classroom" (Norton, 2011, p. 221).

#10—Statement #10 is false. As emphasized in the rationales of Statements #2, #3, and #8 above, the school principal, as learning-leader of the school, cannot permit each teacher "doing their own thing." This is not to suggest that there is no room for teacher autonomy regarding teaching methods, creativity, and using his or her personal strengths in the classroom. A learning culture requires an atmosphere of mutual respect, genuine trust, team effort, and personal commitment to the purposes of the school. No one makes important student achievement decisions on his or her own, including the learning-leader.

Multiple Choice Answers

Response to Question 1: Response "d," *Senior student, Gwen Ryon, wins first place at Regional Student Editorial Writing Conference*, which represents a student's academic success, best represents the view of a true learning-leader. Each of the other choices is a worthy accomplishment in itself. Winning a football championship does represent worthy accomplishments of many student athletes and staff coaches. Academically, however, response "d" focuses on a student learner and centers specifically on academic success.

Response to Question 2: You were asked to list three agenda topics discussed at your last faculty meeting. If your list included a topic dealing with student learning, give yourself credit for a correct answer (e.g., student achievement, academic progress, accountability, learning culture, or achievement data). If your faculty meetings are focused on improving student learning, you are on the right track as a learning-leader.

Response to Question 3: Response "a," *The allocation of time devoted to an issue on both the annual calendar and within the daily schedule*, is the best response. What you talk about, where you spend your time, with whom you associate professionally, your school relationships, and what conferences and workshops you attend all are part of the truest test as to what you truly believe is important. Only response "d" might be a contender. However, the quality of the time spent in developing a school mission and whether or not it results in an emphasis on student learning and a learning culture within the school would determine its importance.

Responses to Question 4: Response "d," *None of the above is similar to the reason I entered the role of school principal*, is a proper choice for a learning-leader. All of the other choices might be the reasons one enters the role, but none reveal the important consideration of the interest in improving student learning and/or the desire to create a learning culture in a school. If you inserted a reason in response "d" that mentioned the words *student learning, student achievement, learning results, learning culture*, or similar terms, give yourself credit for this question. And also give yourself a pat on the back.

Response to Question 5: Response "c," *The regressions likely were due to the fact that these teachers did not fully understand what the data said and how to use the data*, is the best choice in this case. The goal of becoming assessment literate and able to translate assessment results into classroom instruction for students is a difficult task. It isn't enough just to say that teachers need to use data on students' progress to deliver appropriate classroom interventions and learning opportunities. Teachers must understand how this is accomplished. The process required for doing so is discussed in follow-up chapters of the book.

Response to Question 6: Response "d," *Write a note for the record that details the teacher's instructional weaknesses and give the note to him or her for personal reflection*, is not the best way to guide teachers toward improved student achievement. In fact, empirical evidence strongly suggests that the focus on trying to improve teaching performance is far less beneficial than focusing on learning and achievement results. As noted by DuFour (2002), instead of focusing on how to help teachers teach more effectively, it is far more productive to help them focus on improving learning. This concept is discussed in each of the following chapters of the book.

Response to Question 7: Response "d," *Tyler Scott himself*, is the learning-leader's choice in this case. Giving the learner an ongoing opportunity to pursue learning in regard to his or her own personal needs and interests is of paramount importance. Yes, each of the other individuals listed as possible choices might be helpful as a team member. Learning-leaders contend that the individual student has a key role in his or her own learning.

Response to Question 8: Response "e," the personal needs and interests are best determined by the student himself or herself. Empirical evidence strongly supports the fact that student motivation for learning is enhanced if based on personal interest.

Recall the story of Maria presented at the outset of this chapter. Her personal interest in dancing served as motivation for adapting the classroom learning objectives to the topic of dancing. Similarly, a student's interest in low-rider cars or hiking might be used in the assignment of English and spelling lessons. Mathematics and social studies can be tied to either of these two subjects as well. But how can a student know anything about their personal needs? What they need to learn? It will be easy for you to find out. Just ask them.

Response to Question 9: Credit your response as being correct if it was similar to any one of the following word statements: student-centered learning, focus is on the individual student, principals as learning-leaders, focus on achievement results, monitoring of learning progress, personal interests and needs of the student or the school as a learning community.

Response to Question 10: Response "c," *Even if Section 504 of the Rehabilitation Act of 1973 did not prohibit the denial of participation in public education or enjoyment of the benefits of public school programs because of a child's disability, I fully support the concept of an inclusive school whereby each and every child can participate in the normal classroom programs and school activities*, is the choice of a learning-leader. Even though response "d" might lead to positive help for the teacher, response "c" gives a clear message to the teacher that working with all students in classroom settings is part of the principal's learning priorities.

Response to Question 11: Response "c," *Learning is not always sequential and linear*, is the choice response. It is the only response that might help the teacher focus on the student's learning style. Linear learning is contrary to cognitive learning concepts. Encourage the student to keep working and storing new information. Over time new connections are likely to result and insight is likely to occur. One point here is that of learning styles. This topic is discussed later in chapter 4.

Response to Question 12: Response "c," *One term focuses on the improvement of teaching results and the other on student achievement results*, is the best choice. However, give yourself credit also if you selected answer "b." The instructional leader gives primary attention to the improvement of the teacher's performance through classroom observations, performance assessments, in-service programs, clinical supervision, and other activities that focus on improving the teacher. The hope is that the information and skills gained by the teacher will result in improved teaching performance.

The learning-leader gives primary attention to the student and his or her learning results. Emphasis on student achievement is foremost. Progress of the individual student's achievement is monitored, recorded, and analyzed. The data resulting from this procedure are used to determine such matters as the student's achievement progress, methods that either facilitated or inhibited learning results, and what interventions were successful or unsuccessful relative to learning.

Response to Question 13: Response "d," *Just think what our schools are all about; student learning is our primary purpose*, is the choice of a learning-leader. The principal's message makes it clear that changes in the school's environment will be necessary. What has been satisfactory in the past will not suffice in the school's learning culture in the future. None of the other responses is professionally sound.

Response to Question 14: Response "a," *A deep understanding of how humans learn*, is an essential knowledge area for learning-leaders. It supports the concept of individual learning styles and thus underscores the need for the school staff to be cognizant of monitoring learning progress of individual students and the learning methods that were especially successful or unsuccessful. Knowledge of how students learn is a vital component for fostering a learning culture in the school.

Response to Question 15: You wrote a primary reason for applying for a principal's position in a new middle school. There are many reasons why individuals apply for administrative roles. The learning-leader applies for such roles primarily for the opportunity to create a learning culture in the school and to implement a school program plan that is student centered. The primary focus of the learning-leader principal is that of achievement results. If your reason statement included the preceding rationale, give yourself credit for a quality response.

Response to Question 16: Response "d," *Providing leadership for student learning*, is the top selection in answer to Question 16. The other three choices primarily represent management tasks. Each has its own purpose, but learning-leadership is the top priority for realizing student success.

Response to Question 17: Response "a," *Learning-leadership*, of course, is the only appropriate response. Are the questions getting easier, or is your thinking becoming more clear relative to what's important for our schools to achieve? Achievement in what areas are important: reading, math, English, and science only? We don't think so, and this topic is discussed in each of the following chapters of this book.

Response to Question 18: Response "d," *Improve the preparation practices for entering the principalship and focus on instruction and appropriate practice for gaining knowledge, skills, and strategies for improving student learning*, has the greatest potential for helping schools develop a learning culture under a qualified learning-leader.

As stated by Ash and Persall (1999), "Creating an organizational culture and infrastructure that supports leadership opportunities for everyone—a 'leader-full' organization—requires principals to have an altogether different set of leadership skills than have previously been necessary" (p. 1).

As the Institute of Educational Leadership, Inc., has noted, " . . . the school principalship as it currently is constructed—a middle management position overloaded with responsibilities for basic building operations—fails to meet the fundamental priority . . . of leadership for learning or skills needed to meet the challenge" (2000, p. 1). In brief, the principal has received little preparation or support to help him or her deal with the emerging challenges of school-wide leadership for student learning.

Response to Question 19: You were to write a brief response concerning why you were seeking the position of school principal of the largest middle school in the College View School District. At one point in the interview for the position, you were asked how you would demonstrate your accountability as principal of the school.

Give yourself credit for a correct response immediately if you mentioned accountability in terms of providing evidence that each and every student was progressing academically and showing achievement success. Give yourself credit also if you mentioned any of the following accountability measures: holding high academic and behavioral expectations for all middle grade students, providing time and training to support student learning and the standards for instruction set forth by the school and state, monitoring student progress in an ongoing manner to analyze progress results, or moving all students toward proficient performance levels with the goal of closing the achievement gap.

Response to Question 20: Response "a," *School culture is the set of important assumptions, beliefs, values, and attitudes that members of a school and school system share*, is the proper definition of school culture. School culture differs from school climate. This difference is discussed further in a later chapter of the book. In some cases, these two terms are used interchangeably. However, they are quite different. "The culture of an organization allows its members to commit themselves to meaningful purposes and superordinate goals above and beyond personal, vested interests" (Norton, 2008, p. 236).

"School climate is more interpersonal in tone and substance than culture. It is manifested in the attitudes and behaviors of teachers, students, administrators, and community members" (Norton, et al., p. 237). Both topics are discussed comprehensively in other chapters of the book.

You will note that we speak cautiously when discussing the topic of changing the school culture. The terms *culture* and *climate* are often confused in the literature and in everyday use relative to organizational matters. We agree with Gareth Morgan (1986) that an organization's culture is not something that a leader can easily change. Culture is more normative than climate in that it is a reflection of the underlying assumptions of members that go beyond interpersonal relationships. The topic of culture and climate is discussed further in chapter 3.

THE BUILDING OF A LEARNING CULTURE: TRAITS AND BEHAVIORS OF A LEARNING-LEADER

Our purposes in detailing the results of the LLTA exercise included the opportunity to identify many of the behaviors and traits of a principal learning-leader. By examining the rationale related to the responses to the thirty questions and scenarios of the LLTA, several of the traits and behaviors are revealed.

The school principal as a learning-leader:

- **Serves as learning-leader of the school.** Principal learning-leaders understand that their primary responsibility is that of establishing a learning culture in the school. Their focus is that of placing emphasis on student learning and individual student learning results. Chapter 3 centers on this important topic.
- **Gives ongoing attention to the monitoring of student achievement progress.**

    Earlier we noted that "what gets monitored gets done." Many program factors depend on knowing the daily, weekly, and monthly status of a student's progress toward individual and school achievement goals. Knowing what data to collect and how to utilize these findings to assess learning results looms as a significant responsibility of the principal as he or she works with the teaching staff.

    Learning-leaders keep achievement data in front at all times. Data collection and teacher/team analysis of assessment results become part of the school staff's daily work. One analysis concept is that of the "open book" strategy; every grade level "owns" every other grade level. Everything becomes transparent when grade achievement results are examined.

    With assessment data on the table, grade teams make decisions regarding what's best for each student. What changes in subject matter are needed, if any? What teaching approaches might improve the results? Teachers on the team ask, How can I help? Data are used to make instructional decisions. New goals for the student in question are determined. The learning culture of the school is in evidence.

Chapters 2 and 4 extend the discussion of the importance of data analysis in relation to the improvement of student performance. However, Newlund (February 15, 2012) does make us take a step back and consider its impact on creativity and innovations in school programming. Although data analysis is a vital organizational activity, Newlund notes that " . . . it's hard to imagine a business that doesn't also need to create new concepts or offerings" (p. CL1). He alludes to different thinking skills, valuing different sources of information, and remembering that intuitions, concerns, and creative ideas cannot always be supported by a spreadsheet.

Newlund (February 15, 2012) also points out that some authorities caution that our overreliance on data is inhibiting creativity. The need for encouraging creativity and a compelling purpose is of paramount importance for creating innovations and realizing organizational improvements that lead toward the accomplishment of stated purposes.

- **Understands the paramount importance of fostering a positive climate.** A positive climate facilitates working relationships and supports students' interest in assuming a primary role in their own learning. "Many local school districts have reported increases in student achievement following concerted efforts to improve the climate of the school" (Norton, 2008, p. 245). We believe that such research findings are of paramount importance for the work of school learning-leaders. School climate is discussed later in chapter 3 of this book.

    Effective teacher learning-leaders involve students in their own learning in several ways. For example, one strategy for engaging students in their own learning is to ask them, "What is your understanding about a particular topic. What do you know about it?" and "What would you like to know about it?" In this way, teachers are able to engage students in setting their own goals for learning.

- **Stands accountable for student achievement results.** Accountability, as it relates to the work of the learning-leader, is revealed in the extent to which it establishes procedures and initiatives to deal with student learning. In this sense, the programs, interventions, changes, and provisions with objectives of improving student learning are judged according to their ROI (return on investment).

    In a learning culture, the question is not "Did the school principal implement a program based on recommended standards for student learning?" Rather the question of accountability is, "Did the implementation of the program result in the expected standard of student achievement?" or "Did the intervention that was implemented serve to move all students toward higher achievement levels and serve to close the achievement gap(s) revealed in the data collection and analyzing processes?"

    The behaviors and decisions of the learning-leader make it clear that his or her primary purpose centers on student learning and achievement results. Chapter 4 includes a comprehensive consideration of accountability and student achievement results.

- **Gives due consideration to the personal needs and interests of students.** The learning-leader always keeps in mind the student's views of his or her personal interests. Think about this fact for just a minute. You and I both are most satisfied when the work we are doing or the learning that we are experiencing is relevant to our personal needs and interests. What we enjoy as a hobby, for example, is something that gives us pleasure and personal satisfaction.

  One story tells about the motivation of a soldier. Give a soldier a twenty-five-pound backpack and put him on a fifteen-mile hike and he is likely to gripe and complain all the way and back. On the other hand, give him what he really enjoys, a day on the lake for trout fishing, and he will walk fifteen miles to the river carrying twenty-five pounds of food and fishing gear, and he will do so without one word of complaint. A learning-centered school requires an environment where the student can focus on his or her personal interests and strengths.

  Chapter 1 contains many ideas that center on identifying and meeting students' needs and interests. Chapters 2 and 4 provide additional help in this regard.

- **Makes a concentrated effort to increase his or her knowledge concerning how humans learn.** (Note: We plan to discuss the topic of learning styles in detail in chapter 4. Various learning style models will be discussed.) Matching instruction to the learner's learning style gained much popularity in the early 1970s. The mere thought of doing so makes much sense. In recent years, however, the research on learning styles also has received much criticism. A 2009 critique by a reputable psychological science association has found that tailoring instruction to the various models suggested by "authorities" in the field actually produces no better results than not trying to match learning styles at all. Many authorities think otherwise.

  Learning styles refer to the various learning strategies or methods used to help an individual student learn most effectively. The concept of learning styles is having the teacher modify and adapt her teaching methods to the learning style of the student. For example, suppose the teacher discovered that one student learned best through personal experience. The teacher might provide various practical applications of the idea or concept in question. Or in case of a class unit on marketing in social studies, the student might be assigned as a temporary "intern" with a local business. Instead of only reading or studying about something, the student becomes actively engaged in some project.

  We hope that you agree that the importance of student learning still requires the learning-leader and school faculty to do their best to keep abreast of research and best practices concerning how students learn. Chapter 3 and others continue to present ideas relative to students' interests in a student-centered environment.

- **Establishes meaningful strategies for helping teachers acquire the knowledge and skills to become assessment literate.** Learning-leaders must be active in helping faculty and school-community stakeholders understand the achievement standards set by the state and other educational agencies. The principal must be proactive in communicating the importance of establishing clear learning goals and ensuring that all personnel assume their respective roles in the implementation of a learning culture.

Teachers certainly must be assessment literate. Each teacher must become knowledgeable of the various strategies for collecting, monitoring, and diagnosing achievement results. But how is one to determine if he or she or a particular teacher is assessment literate? What is assessment literacy?

Popham (2010) answers the foregoing questions by saying that " . . . an assessment literate educator must be sufficiently familiar with the most significant measurement concepts . . . so that the educator comprehends the essence of those concepts" (p. 1). So if you were asked by a teacher or parent to explain the test validity of the school's achievement test, you would be able to explain that there are several kinds of test validity: content validity, criterion validity, and reliability. A test has content validity, for example, when it measures what it claims to measure.

Empirical evidence has revealed that when the teacher commits to make the classroom a place where learning must take place, student success is likely to follow. Successful results serve to motivate continued efforts by the teacher to ensure individual student achievement. As we have known for years, success breeds success.

In an interview with one school principal, the relationship between success and student achievement was posed. His comment was as follows: "When there is great success in students' achievement results, credit goes to the teachers. When success results are poor, the responsibility goes to the principal." His rationale was that poor success results indicate that he did not give the needed support to the teachers. Do you agree? Why or why not?

When achievement strategies are successful, teachers commonly become teacher learning-leaders. They assume more interest and responsibility for establishing a learning culture in the school by working cooperatively with other teachers on topics of student learning, serving as a mentor for other teachers, serving as a grade level chair, or chairing a school or district curriculum committee.

Chapters 2, 3, and 4 all present strategies for ensuring continued personnel growth and development. Chapter 4 also contains a detailed discussion of accountability as it relates to student achievement.

COMPETENCY-BASED PERFORMANCE AS RELATED TO LEARNING LEADERSHIP

The implementation of state and national standards for student achievement requires the ability to perform specific tasks, implement specific skills, and demonstrate specific evidence that the tasks and skills are being performed and implemented. *Tasks* are those responsibilities, obligations, or requirements to accomplish achievement goals. *Competencies* are those abilities that you need to accomplish a task at a satisfactory level of performance. *Indicators of competency* are the end products or demonstrated evidence that illustrates your ability to perform competently.

Attention to competency performance provides you with a showcase for identifying student achievement tasks of importance and the extent to which you are meeting these tasks in practice. Competency-based performance helps you to define your role as a learning-leader and emphasizes the areas of professional growth required for your best performance.

A comprehensive discussion of competency-based performance relative to your leadership role as a learning-leader is beyond the scope of this chapter. However, see figure 1.2 for an illustration of one task and its competency requirements as related to student achievement.

HOW TO SET STANDARDS FOR STUDENT ACHIEVEMENT

You most likely have received statements concerning student achievement requirements from several different sources including the federal government (e.g., NCLB), state government agencies' content standards, policies of the local school board, recommendations of the local district standards task force committee, and agreements developed by your own local school achievement teams.

Unfortunately, the calls for higher levels of student achievement or additional evidence of achievement accountability commonly are required without the provision of increased human and material resources to accomplish the job. In fact, the current status of the economy might have resulted in a seriously reduced budget for your school operations.

Yet you, as the principal and the school's learning-leader, must continue to give your all to provide the best possible education for every student in your school. Setting achievement standards or doing one's very best to comply with a set of recommended standards is crucial for student learning progress. The learning-leader must continue to hold high expectations for student achievement and provide viable support so that every student has an opportunity to succeed.

HOW FEDERAL AND STATE STANDARDS CAN BE OF HELP

Academic federal and state standards are widely cussed and discussed. You are most likely one of the majority of school principals that dislike the fact that controlling agencies outside the school are controlling much of what is taught in schools today but also

SUCCESSFUL LEARNING EXPERIENCES FOR ALL STUDENTS

Skill	Competencies
1.0 Serve as a learning-leader for the school.	1.1 Ability to establish student learning and academic achievement as the fundamental purposes of the school.
	1.2 Ability to establish achievement requirements for individual students and the school according to national, state, and federal standards.
	1.3 Ability to establish and implement a plan for mapping the current status of achievement results for individual students and the school as a whole.
	1.4 Ability to monitor student achievement progress and use the data appropriately for implementing program interventions.
	1.5 Ability to foster a positive climate in the school that facilitates student achievement.
	1.6 Ability to establish a collaborative climate where all staff personnel work together to identify student needs and interests and then place priorities on meeting these needs.
	1.7 Ability to understand and provide the knowledge of how humans learn.
	1.8 Ability to establish meaningful strategies for helping teachers acquire the knowledge and skills to become assessment literate.
	1.9 Ability to stand accountable for student achievement results.
	1.10 Ability to establish meaningful strategies for helping teachers acquire knowledge and skills to become assessment literate.

Figure 1.2. A Leadership Task and Selected Competencies Related to Learning-Leadership

how well we have to teach it. In some states, a school's label of underperforming, performing, performing plus, highly performing, or excelling is determined by one of the foregoing entities, or perhaps a grade of A, B, C, or failing achievement score is attached to your school. Whether or not federal annual yearly progress (AYP) was met most commonly is answered with a "yes" or "no" response.

We submit that such standards can serve a useful purpose. State and federal standards serve as a beneficial basis for comparing the school's achievement scores with these standards. Standards have served a good purpose in bringing data-based decision making to the forefront. When such standards serve to increase student achievement, we tend to support them.

CHAPTER 1

We have tried to emphasize throughout the chapter that the entire school staff must understand and commit to the school's purposes. Purposes must be accompanied by specific goals and objectives commonly referred to as targets. The targets are based on student proficiency measures on state content standards in the basic subjects of reading, language arts, and mathematics. Principals are able to discern just where the students in their school rank in relation to the overall performance standards of the state. In order to hit the target, it is necessary to understand where your school stands in relation to the academic targets.

Let's assume that 50.0 percent of your fifth-grade students were reading minimally at grade level in 2012 and you set the challenging target to have 100.0 percent of all fifth-grade students reading minimally at grade level by 2019. If an additional 7.2 percent of grade 5 students reached the fifth-grade reading level each year, your school would have reached the intended target.

Some principals that we interviewed were using a similar procedure for monitoring student progress. Only in these cases, each student kept his or her own progress record. Among the benefits for student records were motivation to make some progress each assessment time period and the resulting feeling of satisfaction when assessment results continued upward.

Two very identifiable benefits of such standards are: (1) You and your school staff can determine what students are expected to know and at what level they are expected to perform and (2) Your school curricular program and instruction necessarily must be aligned with the standards that the students must meet. In addition, knowing and understanding the state's content standards provides an opportunity to gain needed consistency in grade and subject matter instruction. It gives your teachers a more confident feeling to know how to "grade" their students' work using more objective assessments. If teachers are to become more objective in assessing students' classroom work, they must increase their own proficiency relative to aligning their instruction with the targets that have been clearly identified. Does this imply "teaching for the test"? We feel more comfortable saying that it is "teaching for the target."

In regard to such high expectations, you are likely to hear many "yeah, buts" from some staff members. "Yeah, but our school is in the lower socioeconomic section of the school district; how can we compete with other schools and be expected to meet the same standards?" "Yeah, but I have several special needs students in my math class; how can I be expected to compete with other math classes?" "Yeah, but I can't be expected to meet individual needs of students when I have thirty-one in my English class." "Yeah, but why am I held accountable for meeting achievement standards that are set by someone sitting in an office in the state capitol building?"

Perhaps there is no satisfactory response that will put an end to such questioning. What we need to keep in mind is that answers to each one of these questions really can help us to be better teachers. The need is to help teachers understand how student progress can be achieved in their situation. Success will serve as the best answer for them.

School principals must implement a vision and a culture for the school in the belief that all students can achieve based on a staff commitment to do "whatever it takes" to make learning happen for each individual.

STEPS FOR REALIZING CONTINUOUS STUDENT ACHIEVEMENT RESULTS

Recommendations for realizing continuous student achievement results were synthesized from interviews and conversations with many practicing school principals. The principals' recommendations correlate quite closely with those of other authorities and agencies that have studied student achievement (California State Department of Education, 2011; School Improvement in Maryland, 2011; ASPEN Institute, 2011; WestEd/MAP, 1999; Georgia Policy Foundation, 2003; and PLC Blog & Discussions, 2011; and others).

You'll want to consider the following common recommendations for realizing continuous student progress:

Recommendation 1. It is a common contention that fostering a cooperative environment in the school is the most important feature for a learning culture in the school. As stated by the Maryland Department of Education (2011):

> Creating a collaborative environment has been described as the "single most important factor" for successful school improvement initiatives. Virtually all contemporary school reformers call for increased opportunities for teacher collaboration. Student achievement is to be greatest where teachers and administrators work together, in small groups and school-wide, to identify sources of student success and then struggle collectively to implement school improvement. (p. 2)

The realization of such an environment for student learning depends on a collaborative group of educators that is convinced that student learning is their number-one priority. Unless you have a magic wand that is working well, the accomplishment of this task will need your best efforts. Chapters 3 and 4 give in-depth consideration to school climate and collaborative teamwork.

In order to accomplish the task of facilitating a learning culture in the school, all of your school rules, administrative decisions, program activities, and school role assignments must center on facilitating quality learning for students. Successful school principals are viewed as leaders that have a strong guiding personal goal that permeates the school and ultimately becomes the school's mission.

Empirical evidence suggests that staff personnel appreciate a leader that expounds a worthy purpose. This is not to imply that you are the sole person that designs the mission for the school. On the contrary, learning-leaders work to foster strong learning-leaders within the school faculty. The vision of a student-centered school must be a shared vision. Each of the following chapters of this book supports this contention.

Recommendation 2. Identifying student needs necessitates the principal's collecting information and specific data from a variety of sources. Teachers and other staff personnel in your school observe student behaviors every day. The school nurse, for example, is a key source for information concerning student health matters. The school counselor is able to assess student attitudes as well as the results of academic and behavioral tests and examinations. Front office staff personnel are confronted with the problems of students in your school on a daily basis.

Of course, your faculty personnel should be instructed to watch student behaviors and changes in their academic performance that should be reported to you and followed up accordingly. This resource bank of school personnel serves an important role in planning and assessing students' academic, personal, and social development. Such information commonly has implications for the academic performances of students.

In summary, you should have information and data in hand from three primary sources: (1) Status reports that provide summary data regarding such measures as academic achievement tests, student attendance data, dropout rates, graduation rates, class performance records for each student, and student interest profiles; (2) AYP data that show how the school and school district have progressed relative to student-group achievement during the school year; and (3) Value-added progress reports that focus specifically on the annual academic progress of each student in your school (Ohio Board of Education, 2011). Each of these three information/data sources will be of great help to you in understanding and supporting your school's student progress.

Recommendation 3. It is the principal's responsibility to make certain that data collected are not only examined and discussed, but are used to adjust classroom instruction that results in student achievement. A data collection process that is presented and discussed but not utilized to plan for needed interventions and changes in the school's curriculum is flawed. We repeat a basic truth: "What gets monitored, gets done!"

You, as school principal, can take the leadership role for arranging opportunities for staff members to talk about achievement data results. Faculty meetings can become learning-achievement meetings. Task force groups and in-service sessions present opportunities for you to use classroom testing results and other achievement data to demonstrate the results of teachers' efforts to improve learning. Increased confidence and commitment to the school's achievement goals are likely to be the result.

Ask yourself several penetrating questions: Are the data needed to make valid decisions about necessary classroom interventions being submitted by all teaching personnel? How often are the collected data being analyzed? Can your teachers interpret the collected data and use the results to modify classroom instruction with their students? Are achievement teams working collaboratively to ensure that the school's achievement standards are being addressed? Are the strengths, needs, and interests of individual students being identified and used to engage them in the learning process?

Recommendation 4. A foundational priority of paramount importance is keeping the school and the school-community focused on and aligned with the primary goal of improving student learning. Your primary benchmark of accountability as school principal is the extent to which you have kept all stakeholders aware and supportive of achievement improvement efforts. Time spent, human and monetary resources expended, collaboration efforts, growth opportunities, and program decisions must be the central focus of your time and effort. Student achievement is the basic element of all education.

In a learning culture, all efforts are made to develop and implement a viable foundation for successful teaching and learning. The school climate encourages collaborative team efforts. Faculty personnel work to make certain that learning plans are implemented and continually monitored. After all, the plan is their plan. School goals and objectives, state standards, and federal guidelines are viewed as ways to guide instructional practices. The school staff views professional growth and improvement as a personal responsibility.

As a leader of learning, you need to possess a research posture. A learning-leader is a consumer, dispenser, and practitioner of action and basic research. True professionals in any occupation pursue, read, think about, discuss, and utilize research information. What would a physician, dentist, lawyer, or chief executive officer of a leading business do without such foundational information to help in the decision-making process? Learning-leaders are no exception.

Authorities emphasize the need for learning organizations to place primary emphasis on being open to inquiry and self-criticism. "For unless an organization is able to change itself to accommodate the ideas it produces and values, it is likely eventually to block its own innovations" (Morgan, 1996, p. 105).

SUMMARY

Maria's story set the stage for the purposes of chapter 1. A teacher learning-leader and a supporting school principal reengaged a student in the learning process by capitalizing on her personal needs and interests. Personal needs and interests, as viewed from the individual student's viewpoint, can be revolutionary in motivating them in ways that will result in continued personal learning progress.

Chapter 1 centered on establishing a foundation for implementing a learning culture in your school. We didn't hand you a magic wand to accomplish this major task. Rather, we asked that you take the LLTA to determine your present status as a learning-leader in your school. But aren't all practicing school principals learning-leaders? Unfortunately empirical evidence points out that many school principals are not prepared to assume this primary role. This fact might have come to the front when you calculated your LLTA score.

CHAPTER 1

But even if your score was good or even excellent, we believe that you will continue to grow and develop as a learning-leader. We submit that the information, strategies, and skills discussed in the remaining chapters of the book will not only serve to verify your current status as a learning-leader but will enable you to strengthen your practice in the leading priority of your principal role: that of further developing the learning culture of your school.

APPLICATION EXERCISES

1. Examine your working calendar for last week (i.e., meetings, phone calls, planning session, student activities, and others). Check the entries that focused on student achievement, the school curriculum, or student learning. Give a moment's thought to your involvement in these activities. Determine a ballpark figure for the amount of time that you devoted to the learning culture of your school. Also think about your leadership role in learning activities during that calendar week.
2. Make a brief review of the major points set forth in chapter 1 relative to maintaining a learning culture in your school. For example, go back to the section in the chapter that dealt with the school principal as a learning-leader. Take a few minutes to judge your personal status on each of the key leadership factors noted in that section on a scale from 1 to 10, 10 being high.
3. Select one idea, recommendation, or comment from chapter 1 that might have made you stop and think for a moment. Why did that entry catch your attention? Is the idea, recommendation, or comment something that you might discuss or just bring to the attention at your next faculty program improvement meeting?
4. During a faculty or team program improvement meeting, place each of the following questions on the board, one at a time. Have the members fill in the blank in each case; then brainstorm their responses. What do the responses have in common? What is the primary focus of the members' responses in each instance, if any? What is the evidence relative to agreements and/or disparities in the members' responses? How might this discussion serve as an eye-opener relative to future discussion about the school's mission and relationships with the community stakeholders and student achievement?
    a. What is your view about school-community partnerships and/or collaboratives? If _____, then I would favor such an arrangement.
    b. What is your view about the accountability measures for student achievement presently being required by the school, state, and other agencies? If _____, student achievement most likely would be improved.

REFERENCES

ALLTHINGSPLC (October 2011). Assessing Principal Performance in a Professional Learning Community. *PLC Blog & Discussions.* Posted by R. DuFour, R. DuFour, & R. Eaker on February 19, 2007. http://www.allthingsplc.info/wordpress/? p=28.

Ash, R.C., & Persall, J.M. (1999). *The principal as chief learning officer,* 84(616), p. 1. Reston, Va.: National Association of Secondary School Principals.

ASPEN Institute (2011). *Improving achievement for all students: Is NCLB accountability producing results?* Atlanta, Ga.: Commission on No Child Left Behind, pp. 1–6. http://aspeninstitute.org/policy-work/no-child-left-behind/reports/improving-achievement-all-students-ncl.

Black, P.J. & Wilian, D. (1998). *Inside the black box: Raising standards through classroom assessment.* King's College London School of Education.

California Department of Education (June 2011). *Recommendations for success: The California Department of Education's 12 recommendations for middle grades success,* http://pubs.cde.ca.gov/tcsii/recsforsuccess/recsforsuccessindx.aspx.

DuFour, R. (2002). Beyond instructional leadership: The learning-centered principal, *Educational Leadership,* 59(8). Alexandria, Va.: Association for Supervision and Curriculum Development.

Institute of Educational Leadership (October, 2000). *Leadership for student learning: Reinventing the Principalship.* A report on the task force on the principalship. Washington, D.C.: Author.

Maryland State Department of Education (August 2011). *Monitoring student progress.* http://mdk12.org/process/student_achievement/Monitor_Student_Progress.html

Maryland State Department of Education (October 2011). *Keep the focus on student achievement.* http://mdk12.org/process/student_achievement/Keep_the_Focus.html.

Morgan, G. (1996). *Images of organization.* Thousand Oaks, Calif.: Sage.

Norton, M.S. (1986). Please not another push to get tough on student retention. *Planning and Changing,* (42) 3/4, pp. 209–223.

Norton, M.S. (2008). *Human resources administration for educational leaders.* Thousand Oaks, Calif.: Sage.

Norton, M.S., Kelly, L.K., & Battle, A.R. (2012). *The principal as student advocate: A guide for doing what's best for all students.* Larchmont, N.Y.: Eye on Education.

Newlund, D. (February 15, 2012). Quantifying data now routine. *The Arizona Republic,* Phoenix, Ariz., p. CL 1.

Ohio Board of Education (October 2011). *Value Added: Module 1: Introduction to value-added assessment.* http://ohiorc.org/value-added/module 1.aspx.

Popham, W.J. (Summer 2010). Assessment illiteracy: Professional suicide, *The UCEA Review,* vol. 51(2).

Robinson, H. (January 2003). *Commentary: Standards-based accountability: Student achievement is the result.* Atlanta, Ga.: Georgia Public Policy Foundation.

Shindler, J., Jones, A., Williams, A.D., Taylor, C., & Cardenas, C. (2003). *Exploring the school climate—Student achievement connection: And making sense of why the first precedes the second.* Los Angeles, Calif.: California State University.

WestEd/MAP (1999). *Impact of standards-based accountability systems,* Chapter 10. Phoenix, Ariz.: Author.

2

Preparing, Organizing, and Enabling the Faculty and Staff for a Learning-Centered School

This book is for you because we believe that you think it is imperative to lead your school toward continuing to be or becoming a learning-centered school. As noted in chapter 1, a learning-centered school stresses quality in all aspects of the school's operations, and its central focus is that of student learning. You want your school's achievement results to reflect high-quality student performance. As Lezotte (1992) made clear, "The changing paradigm implied in the total quality effective school states that schools need to be restructured so that they are organized around student learning" (p. 8).

This statement serves as the foundation for the purposes of this chapter.

PLANNING AND ORGANIZING FOR STUDENT LEARNING

Planning and organizing for student learning requires that you and your teachers give time and serious thought to school operational provisions that facilitate student learning, student performance data, and modeling a learning-centered school. Your goal is to have every faculty and staff person think open-mindedly about becoming even more *learning focused.* You must commit to the goal that every student who arrives on campus realizes that he or she is there to learn, no exceptions.

Your task of getting everyone on the faculty and staff on board the train of student learning is a professional challenge that you can achieve. Your leadership is essential in supporting your faculty, staff, students, parents, and yes, the school community, toward an understanding that "we are all learners." The principal learning-leaders that we interviewed consistently underscored the importance of their activities to learn and share this learning with others.

Angelis and Wilcox (2011) studied schools whose students consistently performed above predicted levels. The purpose of the eight-year study was to ascertain what the school principal, faculty, and staff were doing in order to "beat the odds." They found that high-performing schools shared three common characteristics: (1) teachers, administrators, and staff collaborated and shared responsibility, (2) they made decisions based on a variety of evidence, and (3) their vision of success included high-poverty students achieving beyond predicted levels (p. 27).

LEARNING-CENTERED EDUCATION FOCUSES ON STUDENT LEARNERS

McCombs and Whisler (1997) defined learner-centered education as,

> The perspective that couples a focus on individual learners (their heredity, experiences, perspectives, backgrounds, talents, interests, capacities and needs) with a focus on learning the best available knowledge about learning and how it occurs and about teaching practices that are most often effective in promoting the highest levels of motivation, learning, and achievement for all learners. (p. 9)

Note that the foregoing definition focuses on one key consideration: the student. It encompasses virtually all of the characteristics that loom important in your "getting to know the students." In addition, it emphasizes the importance of using such information for instructional purposes, including how students learn.

As you focus further on the student learner, three basic facts must be considered. First, the students that come to your school and classrooms come at different stages or levels of readiness for learning. Second, a school faculty that focuses on student learning must understand that students come with different backgrounds and have varying levels of motivation for learning. Third, students come to school with an exhaustive range of technological experiences with first-moving and exciting toys such as Xbox, iPod, cell phones, and Wii that may very well be far more exciting to them than when a teacher stands up to lecture supplemented by a PowerPoint presentation.

Each of the foregoing facts underscores information that we have known for years but often have not integrated into our learning methods and practices. Students are different; their needs and interests are different. This fact is further considered later in the chapter.

RECOGNITION OF FAMILY AND HOME DIFFERENCES

Some of your students come to school from a family where one parent is home every day to assist their child with homework, ask questions about the school day, and provide strong support of the teacher's and child's learning experiences that day. On the other hand, other students go home to an empty house and wait for one or both parents to come home. In many cases, the parents are tired from a day's work. Such parents might bring home a fast-food dinner only to settle down in front of the television set too tired to help the child with schoolwork or to ask how the school was that day.

In some instances, the behaviors of parents actually contradict the support that is needed for their child's learning success. That is why it looms important that parental involvement in their child's learning not be optional. Without such involvement, chances of the child's learning success are greatly inhibited.

An important question here is: What should learning look like in a learning-centered school? How is learning facilitated? We focus on the answers to these questions in the following section.

EVIDENCE OF STUDENT LEARNING

Glickman (1993) sets forth several primary provisions that facilitate and provide support for effective learning in an ideal learning-centered school. As you consider each of the six provisions, give thought to how each one applies to your school situation. Or, how might the provision be implemented in your school to enhance student achievement?

Glickman offers the following considerations:

1. Learning should be an active process that demands full student participation in pedagogical, valid work. (Note: What does this provision mean to you? Does the thought that student involvement in deciding about learning activities is of paramount importance come to mind? Does it convey the thought that student learning must be relevant to personal needs and interests?)
2. Learning should be both an individual and cooperative venture where students work at their own pace and at their appropriate performance level. In addition they have opportunities to work with other students in problem-solving situations. (Note: What does this provision mean to you? Does the thought that students must be learning at their personal success level come to mind?)
3. Learning should be goal oriented and connected to the real world. (Note: Does the thought that learning must be purposeful for the student and that the lesson being taught must be viewed as important to the student's present and future needs and interests come to mind? Give consideration to each of the next three learning provisions.)
4. Learning should be personalized to allow students and their teachers to set realistic yet challenging goals.
5. Learning should be documentable, diagnostic, and reflective, providing continuous feedback to students and their parents. Assessment should be used as a tool to develop further teaching and learning strategies.

6. Learning should take place in a comfortable and attractive physical environment and in an atmosphere of support and respect. (pp. 24–25)

The foregoing learning provisions were supported and extended by the Baldrige Foundation (2012). The foundation's learning characteristics, however, give added strength to such considerations as performance assessment processes and student transitions from school to school and from school to work. We suggest that you give thought to each entry as was done with the learning provisions in the foregoing section. Not all recommendations or provisions are appropriate for every school. Nevertheless, each entry might confirm a current practice in your school or suggest a provision that would enhance learning opportunities for your students. Seven of the foundation's learning characteristics for a learning-centered school are as follows:

1. High expectations and standards are set for all students and incorporated into assessments.
2. Faculty members understand that students may learn in different ways and at different rates.
3. A primary emphasis on active learning is provided. This may require the use of a wide range of techniques, materials, and experiences to engage student interest. Techniques, materials, and experiences may be drawn from external sources, such as businesses, community services, or social service organizations.
4. Formative assessment is used to measure learning early in the learning process and to tailor learning experiences to individual needs and learning styles.
5. Summative assessment is used to measure progress against key, relevant external standards and norms regarding what students should know and should be able to do.
6. Students and families are assisted in using self-assessment to chart progress and to clarify goals and gaps.
7. Key transitions, such as school-to-school and school-to-work, are emphasized. (pp. 24–25)

SCHOOL AS A LEARNING ORGANIZATION

Learning organizations provide for learning for every member of the school community; the result is continuous improvement for the school and all its stakeholders. Both learning-leader literature and empirical evidence commonly conclude that, first and foremost, success of the learning-centered school depends on you, the school principal. Learning-leaders are expected to have a sense of clarity, passion, commitment, and purpose in regard to school programs and activities. You must believe that you can make a difference. You demonstrate this belief by setting direction, overcoming obstacles, and refusing to give up. As learning-leader, you maintain a positive tone within the school. Even during tough times, you bring hope to those with whom you work. Others know that the school's goals and objectives will be reached, because your leadership is showing.

In this mode, student advocacy looms important. Advocacy requires a commitment to improve the educational opportunities of all students regardless of their present situation or academic standing. Principal student advocates are student-centered, make decisions that are in the best interests of all students, represent the special needs of all students, stand up for student rights, create school environments in which students can focus on their interests and strengths, are good listeners, and view the school as an inclusive site (Norton, Kelly, & Battle, 2012).

As we emphasize throughout this book, a learning-centered school will have a *shared vision* that encompasses the belief that our school is one where everyone learns. A shared vision provides the opportunity for all personnel and representatives of the school community to be active participants in the school's learning challenges. Saying to students, faculty, and parents that "this is your school" takes on a realistic meaning. Sharing in the vision development creates a common identity that inspires and energizes all to commit to it.

High performance expectations and standards for student learning as well as for school personnel are common benchmarks for effective achievement results. This concept serves to incorporate into the school climate the notion that everyone is a learner and must strive to improve in every aspect of his or her roles and responsibilities at the school.

As previously noted, learning-leader principals structure learning experiences for teachers and students that match their readiness for learning; fit their learning style, rate, and motivation; and organize programs, activities, and experiences that address these considerations. We address these topics later in this chapter and in other chapters of the book. For example, the topic of learning styles is discussed in detail in chapter 4.

Your organizational plan necessarily must include increased attention to student learning results. Both formative and summative assessments must be utilized on a regular and systematic basis to measure student progress. Students cannot be permitted to continue on a level plane of learning and must be challenged to continue on an upward curve toward increased learning and achievement.

You and your teachers must design a plan to collect, examine, and assess student performance data. To what degree are your students progressing in the various subject-matter areas? What areas are showing prominent growth and meeting the required achievement expectations? What subject areas and what students are in need of special attention due to lack of achievement progress? Such questions may be "old hat" in your school experience, but they still remain key questions relative to the status and success of your learning programs and activities.

We have found that collaboration is evident throughout learning-centered schools. In such cases, students are often found working together in groups or teams for

CHAPTER 2

problem-solving activities, tutoring sessions, and coaching sessions. One of the most frequent complaints of teachers in status research studies is that of isolation. Isolation is not a "permitted activity" in the learning-centered school.

Rather, collaborative personnel activities commonly include the examination and analysis of student testing data, identifying areas of strength and weakness, determining intervention needs and/or remediation provisions, and working together to design learning experiences to meet student needs.

Teachers and administrators in high-performing schools in one study attributed their success to meaningful personnel collaboration (Angelis & Wilcox, 2011). In our experience, one of the most effective professional development programs was implemented by a school that created opportunities for teacher teams to meet and discuss curriculum and instruction issues on an ongoing basis.

Not only was the matter of teacher isolation obviated, but idea sharing that often resulted in the need for extended team growth activity was accomplished through the acceptance of growth information on the part of individual members. What was learned by individual team members was brought back to the team for its "learning" as well. Team learning is founded on shared vision and a program of continuous professional growth.

Keep in mind that exemplary learning on the part of students, faculty, and staff is to be shared and rewarded. Learning is to be valued, prized, treasured, coveted, and sought after. Therefore, learning must be rewarded. Figure 2.1 puts the foregoing seven indicators of a learning school into a graphic model. Use the information in the figure to review the important considerations discussed in the foregoing section.

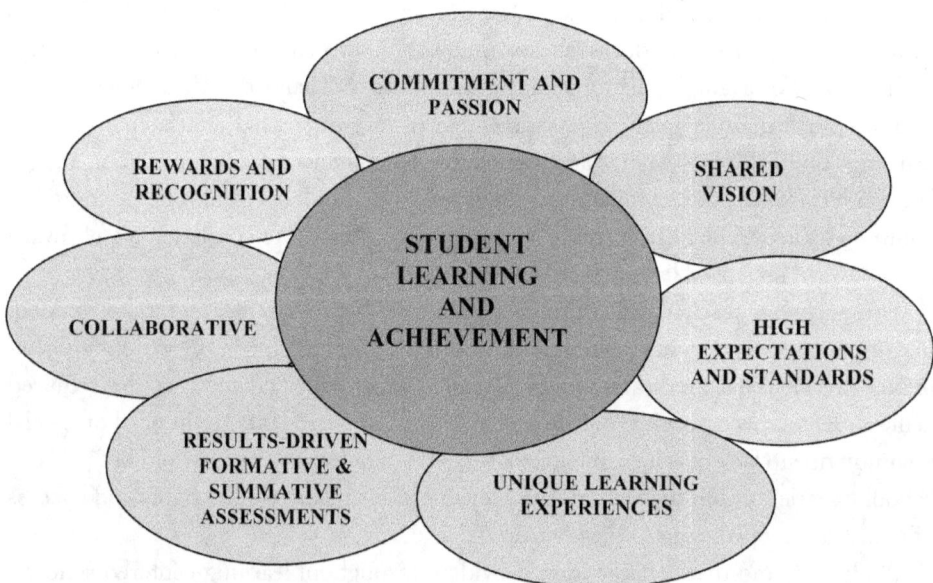

Figure 2.1. Learning-Centered School Major Components

THE ROAD FOR CONTINUING TO BE A LEARNING-CENTERED SCHOOL

School principals throughout the nation are facing the challenges of improving student achievement. Pressures to do so come from many sources. In reality, not much happens toward achieving this goal without the leadership of the person in the principal's office. This is why you most likely took the job; you wanted to make a real difference for students in your school.

Many school leaders already have reached the goal of achieving a school rating of "highly performing" or "A+" regarding student learning. We visited with many school principals who had achieved such ratings; they loved their job but expressed the fact that their job of improving student achievement was not over. Retaining high ratings or realizing even higher quality levels requires continuous improvement.

For those schools that have not yet reached their expectations for a learning-centered school, we ask several questions and then provide recommendations for moving ahead toward higher student achievement goals. The following sections center on initiating steps for becoming a learning-centered school.

RATIONALE FOR BECOMING A LEARNING-CENTERED SCHOOL

Let's assume that you are at the point of wanting to transform your school into a learning-centered school. It makes little difference if you are doing so because it seems that being a learning-centered school is the popular thing to do, that it is something that your colleagues are talking about, or something in your professional bearing that tells you this is why you entered the role of school principal. You still need to give serious thought to several questions or conditions.

Do you have statistical evidence to demonstrate that student learning at your school is not what it should be? This is, do you have data to back up or support your need to move ahead in the direction of a learning-centered school? Are you convinced that this move is the right thing to do in your school's situation? Are you prepared to present data that demonstrate this move to your faculty, parents, and others in the school community?

Are you prepared to counter inaccurate reports of your school's academic performance if and when they occur? Snapshot #1 is one example of a school superintendent's actions when the business community in one school district became disgruntled with reports of the high school's student lack of knowledge of business finance.

Learning Snapshot #1—In a large school district in the state of Kansas, the local Rotary Club engaged a speaker who addressed the topic of educational programs in the field of business management. The Rotary audience consisted largely of local businessmen. Both the local school superintendent and two members of the school board, who were members of the club, were part of the audience.

CHAPTER 2

At one point in the speaker's address, he stated that "In a major study conducted by a named research organization in Florida, it was found that high school students were of the opinion that the profits gained by sales in the business sector were at 200 percent." This statement awakened most every member in attendance; there was audible mumbling among and between members throughout the room.

Although the information and reaction of the club members were embarrassing to the school superintendent and the school board members in attendance, they did not have information at hand to counter the facts of the reported research study and the business profits that were presented. One of the Rotary members in attendance was the local editor of the city's newspaper. He was viewed by most persons in the community as being one of the power influentials in the city. Following the meeting, the editor approached the school superintendent and said, "You need to get on this matter; I have seldom seen the businessmen of this city so upset." The editor of the newspaper, as many in the audience had done, assumed that the research study had included the students at the local high school. How could the high school's students be so misinformed about the realities of business profits?

It was amazing how the negative word of the high school's business program spread among the school community. The school superintendent was fully aware that some follow-up on this matter was essential. First, he called the principal of the local school and asked about the participation of the high school students in the research study. After conferring with the business teachers and guidance counselors at the school, the principal informed the superintendent that none of the personnel could recall any such survey administered to students.

Next, the superintendent attempted to contact the research organization that supposedly conducted the survey but learned that no such organization existed. Other research organizations in Florida were also contacted about their knowledge of such a study. No evidence of such a study in Florida or elsewhere could be found.

At this point, the school superintendent met with the local newspaper editor. He informed him of his investigation of the matter and its lack of results. The editor indicated that it would be of paramount importance for the superintendent to report his findings to the Rotary Club at next week's meeting.

The school superintendent stated that he would be willing to do so, but asked the editor if he would take the time to try to contact the organization that reportedly conducted the study and two other organizations that were knowledgeable about research conducted by state organizations. The superintendent also thought that it would be more objective if the editor reported his findings to the Rotary members. The editor agreed to do so. His calls to Florida resulted in the same findings as the school superintendent's. The so-called research study could not be confirmed, and the named research organization did not exist.

At next week's Rotary meeting, the newspaper editor asked for the floor. In his own way, he made it clear that the information presented at the previous meeting was false; it could not be confirmed. The matter was closed.

The foregoing snapshot is important here for several reasons. One reason is the fact that businessmen and women in every community hold a great deal of interest in the quality of school programs and the status of student learning. Any efforts to make important changes in the school programs are of interest to business leaders; they are a major part of what we have termed the school community. Failure to include them in your efforts to realize a learning-centered school, without the involvement of the business community, most likely will fail.

BUILDING YOUR CASE FOR A SUCCESSFUL VENTURE

We suggest that you consider the following data sources and the areas in which the data have been displayed as shown in figure 2.2. Of course, you will need to complete the information in order to have a good picture of achievement results for your school. For example, you want to compare 2010 eighth-grade achievement scores in mathematics, reading, and language arts with those of the class of 2011. What do the data in figure 2.2 tell you? What conclusions might you draw from such an analysis?

What trends, implications, or achievement gaps can you see within the data? Do the data suggest changes and/or improvements that should be considered?

The data in figure 2.2 give you information that can start you on your way toward establishing a focus on learning in your school. It is clear that the 2011 eighth-grade students performed better in mathematics and reading than the 2010 students. Data reflect the fact that 2011 students performed less successfully than the 2010 eighth-graders in language arts. With such information in hand, you could separate the data into component parts in order to determine achievement gaps that need special attention.

Armed with the many conclusions that can be drawn about your school's achievement status, you are more able to build a strong case for your school to move ahead toward the goal of becoming an improved learning-centered school. You now are more prepared to demonstrate learning trends over a fixed period of time. Areas of strength and weakness are more clearly demonstrated. Data collected from your school can be compared with that of other schools in your school district or state. You have initiated an important first step for becoming a learning-centered school. Best of all, you are now prepared to take the next steps in the improvement process.

THE IMPORTANT PROCEDURES FOR PRESENTING ACHIEVEMENT DATA

Data presentations commonly are given to a variety to school stakeholders. It is of paramount importance that your presentations display important data that challenge and move your audiences toward becoming a learning-centered school. Whatever method

CHAPTER 2

SUMMATIVE ASSESSMENTS	MATHEMATICS	READING	LANGUAGE ARTS
Your School 8th Grade (2010–2011)	87	82	79
Your School 8th Grade (2011–2012)	79	76	81
School District 8th Grade (2010–2011)			
School District 8th Grade (2011–2012)			
State 8th Grade (2010–2011)			
State 8th Grade (2011–2012)			
Your School Dropout Rates (2010–2011)			
Your School Dropout Rates (2011–2012)			
Grade Level Retention Rates (2010–2011)			
Grade Level Retention Rates (2011–2012)			
Class/Subject Repeats			
Dropouts			
Absenteeism			

Figure 2.2. Student Achievement/Performance Data [AQ11]

you choose for presentations should be suited for the audience in question; visuals such as bar graphs, pie charts, and line charts are commonly used to illustrate the important verbal points that you are presenting.

Figure 2.3 is an example of a bar graph that presents scores of sixth-grade students in the school years of 2009–2010 and 2010–2011. Reading scores of the sixth-grade students in the year 2010–2011 significantly exceeded those of the previous school year. Although the data showing the differences in achievement scores are essential, what is needed now is an analysis of the factors that have likely contributed to the differences in achievement.

One approach might be to meet with the teachers of each subject area and determine what the data reveal. For example, the task is to gain the opinions of each group of teachers relative to why there were such significant achievement gains in their disciplines. What factors contributed to the increases in student achievement and what current practices should be continued or increased to ensure continued success? Of course, in those cases when no achievement or decreases in student achievement are in evidence, serious questions relative to the probable factors for these results must be asked.

PREPARING, ORGANIZING, AND ENABLING THE FACULTY AND STAFF

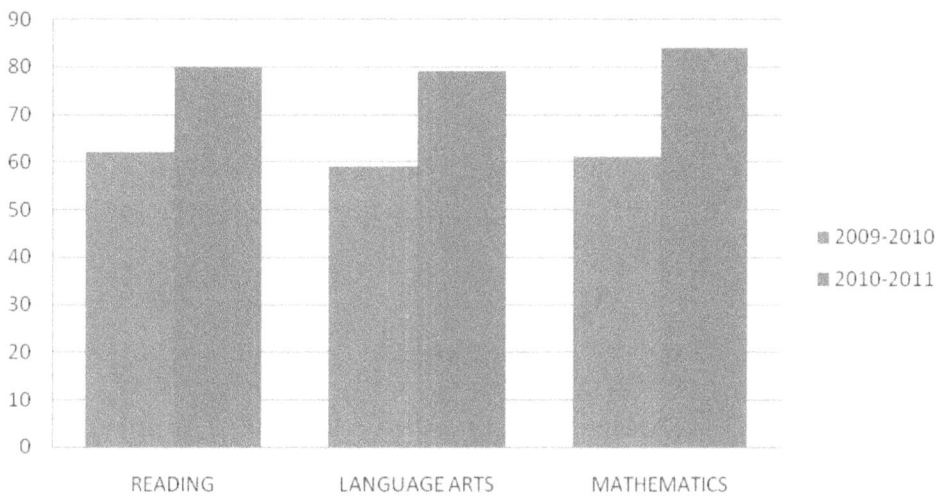

Figure 2.3.

Faculty and staff involvement in the data analysis process has several positive results. Such involvement not only leads to a better understanding of program and student needs academically, but results in a feeling of ownership and ultimate commitment to follow-up program interventions.

CHALLENGING AND MOTIVATING YOUR FACULTY

A major challenge you face as principal is to convey, convince, motivate, and challenge the school stakeholders that the goal of becoming a learning-centered school is one of their professional responsibilities. As noted by Zenger and associates (1994), "If you present your idea as an *intriguing possibility,* not as an obvious improvement that nobody could object to—and if you keep emphasizing the opportunity involved—other people are much more likely to see the future through your eyes" (p. 134).

How do you convince everyone that your school is or can become one where everyone learns? Besides using your magic wand, there really is no simple answer to that question. However, we admired the approach used by one school principal. When he first entered the role of school principal in one instance, he made it clear that he was in favor of an inclusive school arrangement. Regardless of their present status, every child was to be welcomed in the school and placed in the best setting for his or her most successful learning opportunities.

All members of the faculty did not accept the concept of inclusiveness at the outset. Should special needs students be placed with "normal children" in the regular classroom? And how could students with physical disabilities participate in such classes as physical education? Over time, however, faculty personnel became more knowledgeable about working with all students. They witnessed firsthand the learning progress made by gifted students, slow learners, and other students with special needs. Inclusiveness became their personal conviction as well.

The primary focus of your school is student learning, but along with that focus your faculty and staff must become models for learning. Everyone that comes in contact with your school will know that you and your school personnel view student achievement as a primary goal. When anyone walks onto your campus, they must sense an atmosphere of learning. It is your school's primary mission.

GAINING COMMITMENT TO THE PRIMARY MISSION

Your initial orientation of faculty to a learning-centered school concept lies in the selection of new teachers or when experienced teachers transfer to your school. Prior experiences, personal philosophy, and characteristics of student advocacy on the part of teacher candidates loom important. Screening interviews, reference feedback, and specific questions relative to the candidate's views of student learning can serve to prioritize the best candidates for your school. Interview questions should be designed to ascertain whether or not a candidate can assimilate into and make a positive contribution to your school's purposes.

We suggest a few questions that would provide information that would lead you to believe that he or she would be a good "fit" in your school.

1. *At the end of the day, how would you measure your success as a teacher?* You are looking for an answer that incorporates the factor of student achievement and/or accomplishment of learning in regard to curriculum standards. General answers such as "If I feel that I have done a good job" or "Unfortunately, a teacher never really knows if their teaching has made a difference" are unsatisfactory.
2. *What kinds of information do you collect about each student that enables you to determine the extent to which the student is learning in your classroom?* You are looking for an answer that incorporates both formative and summative assessments. That is, what methods do you use to determine if a student has learned what was taught? Or, what activities do you use to ascertain the kinds of follow-up needed for a student in order to reach the required level of understanding needed in the subject?
3. *In what ways have you or might you modify your instruction to accommodate students who are not progressing academically?* You are looking for an answer that incorporates such options as specialized grouping of students, verbal or written assignments, varied assignments, or special tutoring. The primary consideration centers on the candidate's realization that student performance results always give clues to interventions and/or other appropriate follow-up as soon as possible.
4. *What experiences have you had in collaborating with others in designing alternative educational options for students who need additional help?* You are looking for

an answer that incorporates some form of teamwork or collaboration with other professional personnel. In the case of candidates with no prior teaching experience, student teaching experiences in this area would be appropriate. If no prior experience is reported, a follow-up question might be to simply gain the candidate's thoughts regarding working with other teachers concerning their questions about teaching and student results.

5. *What would be the most important thing that you as a classroom teacher could do in order to ensure that every student achieves the desired learning for a student?* You are looking for a response that includes thoughts about student learning, student needs and interests, teacher-student relations, data collection and analysis, and so forth. If the candidate states that he or she is the one responsible for ensuring that every student achieves, more weight should be given the answer.

THE MAJOR TASK OF ORIENTING THE FACULTY AND STAFF

You will have to determine the best time and method for introducing the concept of the school as a learning center, perhaps a new direction, to your faculty, staff, and school community. You could begin with grade level chairs, department chairs, your parent or site-based council, the school's leadership team, or perhaps the entire faculty and staff. Whatever method you choose will require that you give extensive thought to those characteristics that are research based, inspiring to your audience, and will produce the desired results. Perhaps the model previously presented will help you get started (see figure 2.1).

Figure 2.1 presents major components of a learning-centered school. All of the components are conditioned by the central focus of student learning and the results of student achievement. If your school has already established a viable school vision, then the establishment of the school's expectations and standards for academic achievement is a logical place to start. If a meaningful school vision statement has not been established, such a guiding statement must be developed with the full commitment of the faculty and staff.

IN-DEPTH ANALYSIS OF STUDENT ACHIEVEMENT DATA

In regard to faculty and staff orientation, we suggest that your preparation for this effort begin with learning all that you can about the academic performance of students in the school. We believe that hard data concerning the current performance of your students are essential for determining your school program's strengths and areas needing attention. You will utilize the data to draw conclusions about the efficacy of current program provisions, make judgments about needed improvement steps, and drive decision making relative to best program interventions and provisions. As Collins noted (2001), "The good-to-great companies displayed two distinctive forms of disciplined thought. The first . . . is that they infused the entire process with the brutal facts of reality" (p. 69). Hard data, whether good or bad, constitute the brutal facts of reality of student learning in your school.

STUDENT ACHIEVEMENT DATA ON DISPLAY

You will be collecting and analyzing data, drawing conclusions, and displaying data from a variety of student performance assessments. Data gathered can be prepared as visuals suitable for handouts to appropriate groups and for use in group discussions. Data will be the heart of your case for commitment to the challenges of reaching your goal of a learning-centered school.

Consider the following suggestions for presenting your data. In any handout developed, one graph or chart per page is recommended. In that way, the reading or listener focuses only on that display. Next, it is best that only one disaggregation per page be considered. For example, if comparing math scores of sixth-grade students, display the scores by gender only. Be sure that each axis or segment of a graph or chart is clearly labeled. Make graphs and charts simple for ease of understanding. It is essential that findings, what the data reveal, are clearly stated.

Empirical evidence suggests that it is best to present school data first to your leadership team or other in-school groups or committees. In this way, any concerns on the part of faculty personnel can be properly addressed and perhaps corrected. At this point, input from knowledgeable individuals and groups should be welcomed. Such action on your part adds to the goal of collaboration and sharing of decision making on the part of your school personnel.

TOWARD THE GOAL OF ESTABLISHING TEACHER LEARNING-LEADERS

The concept that everyone in the school is a role model of learning must be emphasized. Everyone is a learner and each student in the school is the responsibility of every teacher. Without the commitment and participation in the activities necessary for establishing and maintaining a learning-centered school, the goal cannot be fully accomplished.

Expect your teachers to continue to learn as you learn with them. Which methods, strategies, and lessons are most effective? Expect your teachers to build on those methods that are producing best performance results, expect them to discard or modify those that are not. Each teacher is expected to know their students and to continue to keep abreast of the academic performance of students that were in their classes previously. What a teacher might have learned about a student's learning style should not be kept a secret, rather such information should be passed to other teachers who are now working with the student. The topic of student learning styles is discussed later in chapter 4.

Office and maintenance personnel are to be included as learners as well. Everyone on the faculty and staff must see the connection between their job responsibilities and the accomplishment of the learning goals established for the school. For example, office personnel are always looking for more efficient, systematic and orderly procedures to process student requests such as initial class placement. Maintenance personnel must understand the importance of a clean, attractive, and well-maintained school in relation to the school's image as a learning center.

ASSESSMENT OF PROGRESS TOWARD DESIRED PERFORMANCE RESULTS: STRETCH GOALS

A learning-centered school has established progress standards and goals. Welch (2001) refers to *stretch goals* where individuals " . . . reach for more than what you thought possible" (p. 385). The learning-leader continually searches for ways to stretch the expectations and academic achievement levels of students.

We endorse the concept of stretch goals and encourage you to challenge your teachers and staff to establish such goals for themselves and their students. *Let's achieve the impossible* would be an appropriate motto. Teachers in effective schools assume the attitude of "never good enough and their stance toward change is to expect it, respect it and, by continuous progress monitoring try to cause it" (Wilcox & Angelis, 2011, p. 29).

As a learning-leader, you must take the lead in identifying needed changes in your school's program and begin to explore with teachers and staff personnel about steps to take in order to respond to those changes.

But what about school district policies and regulations that you must face? Effective school leaders do not merely accept all the rules and regulations of their school districts. Rather, reportedly they always test the limits in an effort to change those things that are not favorable to student learning (Mazarella & Grundy, 1989). We've never said that effective learning-leaders do not have to have courage of their convictions. On the contrary, proactive behaviors and courageous stands are two characteristics that you will need to serve as a true learning-leader.

Statewide performance standards for students prevail across all states, and schools are expected to meet the standards. Most state standards are accompanied by local school district standards. In a learning-centered school, additional progress standards are set for each student. Such standards commonly are referred to as benchmarks for expected student progress. Measuring student progress against the benchmarks gives the teacher useful information for deciding the content of the next lesson and/or the most appropriate instructional methodology.

Not only is it important to set benchmark goals for each learner, goals must set clear and appropriate benchmarks for the school. These *improvement goals* center on what you and the school faculty want to accomplish in order to improve the school programs that better suit students. Two or three meaningful goals will suffice. As noted by Lezotte (2002), "Fewer goals usually have a better chance of succeeding than many goals" (p. 174).

A basic principle of learning-centered schools is that "we will provide relevant curriculum experiences for all students." This principle implies that learning experiences and activities will be determined in the best interests of each individual student, specifically his or her personal needs and interests. This requires the teacher to systematically collect, analyze, and use student performance data for making instructional decisions for students.

EXPECTATIONS OF STUDENT GUIDANCE AND COUNSELING SERVICES

A component of the learning-centered school that is often overlooked is the role of the guidance counselor in providing encouragement, support, and guidance to students. Counselors are expected to help students understand and deal with social, behavioral, and personal problems that they face. Emphasis is to be placed on preventive and developmental counseling. Student self-direction relative to personal, social, and academic growth is the desired result. " . . . Students need to be held accountable for their own 'poor choices' or 'poor judgment'" (Norton, et al., 2012, p. 19), but the student advocate understands that approaches to student discipline are most effective from the perspective of student learning as opposed to punishment being the best solution. Effective guidance counselors are student advocates. They serve to support student rights and practice nonpunitive discipline methods.

We expect counselors to work collaboratively with teachers, parents, principals, school psychologists, and other professionals in helping students succeed. Of much importance, however, is for counselors to work closely with classroom teachers when dealing with students' needs, problems, and issues. Neither counselors nor teachers should work in isolation. Why? Because doing so is contrary to the best interests of students and successful learning results.

Effective collaboration between and among professional school personnel requires that every faculty and staff member *jump on board* to make the school a better school. We take the position that learning-centered schools cannot tolerate obstructionists. As Collins (2001) has stressed, good to great leaders "first got the right people on the bus, the wrong people off the bus, and the right people in the right seats" (p. 13).

We believe that all teachers really want to be better teachers. In some instances, the thought of having to change inhibits their acceptance of new interventions and different procedures. In some cases, the individual's ego-defensive mechanisms will not allow them to admit and face their weaknesses.

We do have some suggestions in this and other chapters of the book for dealing with these dilemmas. However, our best advice at this time is to find out about the teacher's key interests and strengths and see that they are implemented in the activities that they must perform. You can learn much about one's interests and strengths by observing their behaviors. Perhaps the best way to gain this information, however, is simply to ask them.

DON'T OVERLOOK THE PARENTS

We have pointed to the importance of parent involvement throughout this book. Few program changes in your school will be successful without the understanding and support of the students' parents. We were impressed by the statement of one school principal set forth in the foreword of the school's publication, *Ward Traditional Academy 2011–2012 Parent Handbook*. We thought that we would share her statement with you.

> Dear Parents of Ward Traditional Academy,
>
> As we move into our seventh year as a school in the Tempe Elementary District we continue to grow and change to meet the needs of our learners and parents. We are looking forward to another successful year of learning and growing as a school and community. As you read through your *Parent Handbook* and use it as a reference tool throughout the year, I hope the importance of your role in your child's education permeates throughout. Ward Traditional Academy has made a strong impression both in our district and in our neighborhood. It is through continued support of our parents, staff, and community that we will continue to be successful in our educational endeavors. Again, please consider this letter as an open invitation to share your thoughts and ideas with me so we can continue to provide the highest quality education for our students. Thank you for your continual support of your students, our staff, and our school.
> Your Partner in Education,
> Kacy S. Tomason
> Ward Traditional Academy Principal (Used by permission, p. 9)

EQUIPPING THE FACULTY AND STAFF FOR A LEARNING-CENTERED SCHOOL

Training and Professional Development

Although school personnel commonly want to serve effectively in a learning-centered school, unfortunately many of them have not been adequately prepared to do so.

CHAPTER 2

Equipping the faculty to succeed in a learning-centered school then becomes a major responsibility for the principal. The central focus of professional development for faculty personnel centers on the question, *What must a teacher know and be able to do in order to be an effective teacher in a learning-centered school?* The answer to this question provides the foundation for an effective professional development program for your faculty.

We suggest that information on the topic of individual learning styles looms important. We discuss the topic of student learning styles in depth later in chapter 4. We stress throughout the book that teachers must understand how to collect student achievement data and how to analyze such data and use it to improve their classroom teaching.

One principal stated that teaching teachers how to analyze student performance data and be comfortable using it was the most important first step that needs to be taken. In this situation, teachers at her school met during their preparation periods each day to review student assessment data. In the follow-up, adjustments were made in instructional methods to accommodate students, especially those students who failed to meet the required academic standards.

We argue throughout this book that the best professional development is self-development. "Each individual must assume the primary responsibility for his or her own continuous personal growth. When this occurs, a school system truly begins to demonstrate the characteristics of a learning organization whereby the needs in the system are readily identified by the system personnel and the personnel initiate steps to correct or improve the identified concerns" (Norton, 2008, p. 196).

THE LEARNING-CENTERED SCHOOL AND LEARNING TO LEARN

Gareth Morgan (1986) provides excellent models for considering the procedures of a learning organization. Note, especially, how closely Morgan's concepts tie to our discussion of collecting student performance data, analyzing the data, and then taking the necessary steps to utilize the information to improve current practices.

Morgan's (1986) *single-loop learning model* begins with step 1, the process of sensing and scanning the environment to detect the present status of performance in the system. Step 2 involves the comparison of the information found in step 1 with the organization's stated norms or standards. In step 3, the process of questioning whether the operating norms or standards are appropriate is answered. For the final step 4, the process of determining and implementing appropriate follow-up action is determined.

Morgan's idea of *double-loop learning* takes the concept of organizational learning one step further. His step 5 focuses on the question: Are operating norms or standards correct? Morgan is quick to point out that double-loop learning is more difficult and elusive than single-loop learning. That is, for many existing organizations, including schools and school systems, encouraging ongoing debate and challenging basic norms, policies, and operating procedures in relation to changes commonly is accompanied by criticism and even claims of insubordination.

With these thoughts in mind, let's consider briefly three guidelines for approaching the development of the learning organization, in our case the school (Morgan, 1986):

1. Encourage and value an openness and reflectivity that accepts error and uncertainty as an inevitable feature of life in complex and changing environments.
2. Encourage an approach to the analysis and solution of complex problems that recognizes the importance of exploring different viewpoints.
3. Avoid imposing structures of action upon organized settings. Rather than imposing goals, objectives, and targets, it is important to devise means where intelligence and direction can emerge from ongoing organizational purposes.
4. Make interventions and create organizational structures and processes that help implement the above principles. (pp. 94–95)

FACULTY TEACHING FACULTY

Another strategy for equipping the faculty for learning is to schedule systematic and periodic presentations on relevant topics and issues that they face. Some principals set aside time before each faculty improvement meeting to provide these types of in-service. For example, a faculty member or team of members could take the component Unique Learning Experiences that was presented previously in figure 2.1 and elaborate on the different learning experiences they provided for students in need of some alternative instruction.

The foregoing activity satisfies another component of the learning-centered school, namely, rewards and recognition. Presenters are recognized for their achievements in providing a worthwhile service to other faculty members. More schools appear to be implementing early release days when faculty members get together to address specific learning issues and trends that the assessment data revealed during analysis sessions.

More schools are also changing the traditional faculty meeting to learning improvement work sessions. Such meetings serve several purposes, including opportunities for collaboration, reduction of teacher isolation, focusing on relevant learning issues as opposed to information dissemination sessions, and reinforcing the school's mission as a learning-centered school.

A COLLABORATING FACULTY AS A LEARNING FACULTY

As we have stressed throughout this chapter, collaboration is essential to ensure student academic success. In a learning-centered school, faculty and staff members collaborate to determine what students are in need of special attention and then work together to design and implement strategies to meet those needs.

In his book *Mastering the Art of Creative Collaboration,* Hargrove (1998) quoted John Seely Brown, chief scientist at Zerox's Palo Alto Research Center, as saying that "Knowledge is a social activity. Complex problems cannot be solved by specialists thinking and working in isolation, but in coming together through a process of dialogue, deeply informed by human values that are grounded in practical problems" (p. xii).

You must expect that faculty members come together to address, diagnose, and resolve student-learning issues in a collegial atmosphere. When all individuals use their personal knowledge, skills, and strengths in collaborative activities, they come to realize that goals can be reached that might not have been reached on their own.

When and how should collaboration be done? Right now, according to Hargrove (1998). Hargrove says that for you to become a collaborative leader, you need to begin right now thinking differently about yourself as (1) a visionary leader, a creator . . . instead of thinking of yourself as an employee, (2) someone who can bring an extraordinary combination of people together and create some real value, (3) working on something you are really passionate about, (4) being a great team leader and supportive colleague, (5) being part of living network . . . where even the smallest action can spread out and have far-reaching consequences, and (6) a person creating something together with other people within an immutable timetable and budget (pp. 49–50). Why not put yourself under the microscope of those preceding ways of thinking about yourself?

You might find it of value to develop a worksheet such as the one set forth in figure 2.4. Identify your behaviors that you believe contribute to becoming more collaborative. For example, consider the first cell, Visionary Leader, and identify the behaviors that you believe you presently exhibit. What behaviors might be added to your list in order for you to become even more collaborative? You might enter such things as: Ask others for their opinions. Visit with others about joining you in the completion of an ongoing learning project. Meet with two or three faculty or staff personnel to solve a current problem.

Just how open are you about your present status as a collaborative leader? Are you willing to ask others to complete an assessment of yourself as a collaborative person? Stress the importance of "brutal honesty" as well as anonymity. Such feedback certainly would give you some idea of your status as a collaborative person. Just your openness about asking for such input most likely would impress the school's faculty and staff.

If the foregoing activity goes well, you might want to extend it by asking members of your learning leadership team or appropriate group to complete the same activity individually. As principal, consider listing all of the behaviors that you and the team or group identified for each characteristic in figure 2.4. The list should serve as a realistic reminder for you and others relative to incorporating the "contributing behaviors" into daily operations and activities in the school. The list might serve you well as a staff development tool for yourself and faculty.

PREPARING, ORGANIZING, AND ENABLING THE FACULTY AND STAFF

CHARACTERISTICS OF A COLLABORATIVE PERSON	MY BEHAVIORS TO BECOME MORE COLLABORATIVE
VISIONARY LEADER	
BRING EXTRAORDINARY PEOPLE TOGETHER	
STUDENT LEARNING IS SOMETHING I AM PASSIONATE ABOUT	
TEAM PLAYER AND SUPPORTIVE	
MY LIVING NETWORK(S)	
SOMETHING CREATED WITH OTHERS	

Figure 2.4. Collaborative Person Assessment

COLLABORATION—MUCH MORE THAN JUST MEETING AND TALKING

The topic of collaboration enters the discussion in several instances in this book. We emphasize the topic in this chapter and again in chapter 4 when we approach it from the perspective of viable partnerships. Collaboration must be more than conversations between and among school personnel. Rather, effective collaboration is a proactive phenomenon that is undergirded by purpose. In relation to learning and student achievement, its purposes must result in better understandings, better relations, better teaching, and better academic performance results.

One of the landmark books on the topic of collaboration is R. A. Hargrove's work, *Mastering the Art of Creative Collaboration* (1998). This author speaks of the seven blocks of collaboration that include proactive actions of reinventing yourself, seeking out strategic partners, building shared goals, designating clear roles, spending time in dialogue, creating shared work places, and focusing on zest factors. We recommend that you obtain a copy of Hargrove's book for the school's professional library. Although it is not possible to present all of the useful ideas related to Hargrove's seven blocks in this chapter, let's look at one of these blocks, that of *zest factors*.

A zest factor, according to Hargrove (1998), is a factor that "elicits a compelling challenge, a sense of urgency, near and clear success, spirit of collaboration, self-organization,

SCHOOL-WIDE CHARACTERISTIC	FALLING SHORT	ACCEPTABLE	GREAT JOB
Administration, faculty, and staff demonstrate a high level of interest, commitment, and energy toward achieving school goals.			
Collaboration exists between and among faculty, staff, and administration when addressing school and/or student problems, issues, or concerns.			
The school's vision is discussed both formally and informally by all faculty and staff.			
Student performance/achievement data are collected, analyzed, and used to make decisions on a regular and systematic basis.			
We recognize and reward individuals (students, faculty, and staff) for demonstrated contributions to ongoing student achievement.			
Expectations and standards are continuously being evaluated, and student performance in relation to the standards is continuously assessed.			
Learning experiences for students are periodically revised in line with student needs as determined by student performance data.			

Figure 2.5. Learning-Centered School Self Assessment

pride of achievement, fear of failure, experimentation, ignoring documentation, and taking action" (p. 107). In a school situation, a zest factor might be an unfortunate finding that there was a significant drop in reading scores on the statewide assessment tests between fourth and fifth grades. Such an event conjures up a sense of urgency and a fear of failure and yet a motivation to take some action.

On the other hand, a zest factor might be a notable increase in the number of parents who are volunteering to serve in the school in whatever capacity they may be needed. Such an event brings about a spirit of collaboration and pride in achievement.

Positive zest factors suggest a time for celebration. They also suggest a time for reflection. For example, teachers in a classroom where students demonstrated growth in formative assessments over a grading period would be asked to reflect on just why this zest factor occurred; what was done differently during the grading period that influenced the positive result?

Learning Snapshot #2—Visualize faculties at two different high schools that determined the zest factor, *Tardiness in these schools was a horrible interruption of instruction at a critical time in the class period.* In regard to building shared goals, the two schools faced the problem of remedying the tardy problem. They were determined to end the problem of excessive tardiness within the next month.

The two high school faculties minimized the tardy problem by implementing two different strategies. At one school a plan called "sweep" was implemented. Teachers who were on their preparation period and the security staff were out on the campus and swept it for straggling students. Straggling students were taken into a holding room and remained there for the entire period. They were not permitted to go to their locker to get their class materials. The students soon learned that sitting in the holding room was a penalty that they did not want to pay. Each student had to take much extra effort to catch up with the class missed. Thereafter, they made it a point to get to class on time.

At the other high school, the tardy bell was eliminated. Teachers began classroom activities independently of other teachers. The result was that students ceased to rely on the tardy bell and reported to classes before each teacher started the lesson. This practice eliminated the practice of students congregating in the hallway just before class began and rushing late to the classroom after the tardy bell had rung.

In both cases, the "sweep" and the "no tardy bell" strategies were designed and developed in a collaborative setting that included teachers, counselors, and administrators.

"Yeah, but those strategies wouldn't work in our school situation," you might contend. That's not really the point here. The point is that a zest factor faced the two schools; they had determined where they were now and that the negative factor of student tardiness was inhibiting student learning. They asked themselves, "Where do we want to be one month from now concerning this matter?" The answer was that of getting rid of all tardiness in the school situation. They answered the important question of "How do we get there?" by meeting and agreeing on a plan of action that was successful when implemented. Did the strategies implemented serve the intended purpose of influencing student achievement in a positive manner? Future achievement assessments would have to answer that question.

We extend the consideration of developing and implementing a school plan for learning improvement in the following section. Based on the questions of where we are now, where we want to be, and how we will get there, you and your faculty will develop a plan for improving learning at your school.

DEVELOPING AND IMPLEMENTING A VIABLE PLAN FOR LEARNING IMPROVEMENT

You might be saying to yourself that we already have a learning improvement plan in place. If this is the case and your plan has proven successful, you are to be congratulated. It's time for celebration. However, the following discussion might still be beneficial for you in reviewing your current plan and perhaps making improvements. In either case, an initial step in your plan for either reviewing your present plan or developing and implementing a new plan for learning improvement is to assume the task of completing a school profile. Such a profile is a mapping procedure that reveals the status of student achievement results at the present time.

Consider assigning the task of developing a school profile to a group of teachers, a profile committee, who are highly skilled and thoroughly enjoy working with assessment data. Explain to them the need for determining exactly how well the students are performing by using a variety of assessments that will serve as the basis for developing school goals and academic standards. This procedure necessitates the identification of achievement data already in hand as well as other performance data that is important to the task. A data profile is developed using the information gained from state-wide tests, district-wide tests, teacher tests, demographic data, surveys of parents, and school graduates and other sources.

After a close examination of the school's profile, a collaborative effort to develop appropriate student performance learning goals and standards looms important. Often this task is accomplished by having the faculty work in teams. Teams are assigned commonly by grade levels, subject-matter areas, or by the special interests of faculty members. Such an arrangement has a number of benefits. It gains the combined intelligence of teachers in your school and leads to the important factor of commitment to the standards on the part of the participants.

GETTING THERE—THE SCHOOL'S IMPROVEMENT PLAN

Once the school has established its learning goals and standards, it is a common practice to assign faculty teams to design plans for implementing the goals. Perhaps one primary goal should be assigned to each team. Each team is given the responsibility for developing plans for achieving the goal. Such a responsibility includes (1) the interventions appropriate to the goal, (2) relevant and timely assessments of student progress, (3) systematic analysis of student progress, (4) faculty discussions on the results of the analysis and recommended strategies for closing identified learning gaps, and (5) implementation of the strategies determined by the team.

SCHOOL-WIDE IMPROVEMENT PLAN

Each student-learning goal is incorporated into a school-wide improvement plan. We make note of the fact that schools in many states are accredited by organizations such as AdvancEd, the National Independent Private Schools Association, New England Association, or the Independent Schools Association of the Southwest. These associations often have their own templates for school improvement planning.

Developing clear goals and responsibilities applies to the implementation of the improvement plan to achieve the goals set for the school. The strategy here is to identify specific steps that need to be accomplished and then allow the faculty and staff personnel to select those steps that best match their interests and talents. For example, one person might enjoy monitoring the implementation plan and keeping a record of tasks, responsibilities, and timelines. Another faculty or staff member might wish to serve as recording secretary and prepare minutes of meetings for dissemination.

ENABLING THE FACULTY AND STAFF FOR OPTIMAL PERFORMANCE

You must take the initiative to enable the faculty and staff to function effectively in the learning-centered school environment. This task begins with acquiring and providing the resources needed for instructional purposes.

Human Resources Needs

The principal serves not only as a role model for learning but also as a source for providing essential resources. Human resources such as paraprofessionals, teacher aides, student assistants, and community volunteers are of vital importance for meeting the learning needs of students. Paraprofessionals, teacher aides, and additional staff require budgetary considerations whereas volunteers and students aides do not. Student assistants are resources often overlooked. When a talented student is asked to serve as a student mentor for another student, both students benefit.

Your community itself will have a variety of human resources that might work cooperatively with your improvement plan. In chapter 4, we address the topic of collaborative partnerships with community agencies and individuals. Give full consideration to such resources that can serve you well by volunteering their services or providing certain material resources for use in your program activities. If you have not already done so, you'll be surprised at the positive responses received in this regard.

We mention in this book the practice in one elementary school that requires parents to provide a minimum of twenty hours of volunteer service to the school each year. In a school of 300 students, this requirement adds approximately 6,000 hours of parent services for the school each year. If such a "requirement" is not plausible in your situation, think about recommending an acceptable number of hours expected for parents to work with their child each week at home. Most every parent wants what is best for the child's education. Although some parents will not or are not able to provide such service, you'll find that the large majority of parents will meet or exceed the request.

CHAPTER 2

Time as a Resource

Time for planning and collaboration between and among faculty members is an invaluable resource. Scheduling a common preparation time that enables teachers of the same grade or subject area to meet, discuss, and plan is a must. One principal stated that teacher preparation periods were used to analyze student benchmark assessments and determine specific learning activities to bridge any achievement gaps. Establishing teacher learning improvement days, early student dismissal days, and utilizing such programs as scientists for teacher days provide excellent opportunities for regular classroom teachers to concentrate on improving learning activities.

Class Size

Reducing class size has been one of the most discussed topics in education. Opinions concerning the effects of class size on student learning are mixed. Class size has been a dominant concern as it relates to teacher load. Studies of teacher load indices have shown that some teachers have load indices two to three times that of other teachers (Norton, 2008, p. 9). One major study of class size (Glass & Smith, 1978) concluded that small classes of approximately ten students do result in higher levels of student achievement. Some states and the federal government have enacted legislation to reduce class size.

Our suggestion is that you carefully analyze student performance data and determine if it suggests a reduction in class size in any class or subject area. Such an analysis might also suggest a variety of alternatives for organizing class arrangements including class size. For example, other alternatives might include team-teaching arrangements, peer tutoring, distance learning, ungraded classroom organization, computer-assisted instruction, or other technologically based assistance.

Minimizing Classroom Interruptions

Are you aware of the average number of times that your classroom teachers are interrupted in various ways during their instruction? We do not have specific information of the statistics in this regard, but believe that ensuring efficient school operations that minimize the interruptions of the teaching/learning environment is highly important. One school faculty decided that there would be no instances when students would be called from class other than emergency situations. Parents were informed of the school's regulation on this matter. Students were called to the office only during a recess, before or after school, or during study hall.

Minimizing classroom interruptions placed a noticeable emphasis on the importance of teaching and learning. In the case of the school mentioned above, in a very short time all school personnel became use to the process and functioned more effectively under the no-interruption ruling.

SUMMARY

This chapter focused on two primary purposes: (1) to engage you in a serious process of self-reflection and (2) to give you relevant information for engaging and transforming your school into a learning-centered environment. We wanted to have you rethink your role as the learning-leader of the school and to ask yourself several reflective questions: Are all of the students in my school achieving and experiencing success in all aspects of their school life? Are students learning what has been determined as essential by our learning improvement plan? Am I doing everything in my role to make our school a school where everyone learns?

Relevant information regarding strategies for engaging your staff into the process of improving or transforming your school into a learning-centered school was discussed in-depth. Two areas of emphasis included the importance of student achievement data in determining program needs and assessing the effectiveness of ongoing programs and interventions.

Leadership behaviors needed, when introducing your faculty and staff to the concepts of change, were emphasized. Collecting achievement data from a variety of sources, using teams to analyze the data, and establishing follow-up procedures for implementing needed program changes and interventions were considered.

In the chapters that follow, many of the learning-leader concepts introduced in this chapter are extended. The importance of data analysis, learning climates, collaboration, and student learning styles are among those concepts that will be discussed additionally in later chapters.

APPLICATION EXERCISES

1. Deciding how to begin your move toward a more focused school for student learning entails a number of strategic decisions. One such decision is that of collecting and analyzing student performance data and drawing conclusions relative to positive or negative trends or gaps that need attention.

    With some appropriate data in hand, schedule a time for teachers to meet and consider the data in terms of what the data tell them. Next, ask them what the data mean in terms of improving student learning. In what areas, subjects, or grade levels does it appear that positive program practices are producing positive achievement results? In what areas does it appear that some changes are necessary? Ask what they see as the next steps. What should we do next? Where do we go from here?

2. Planning and preparing your personal activities serves to move your school forward to becoming more focused on student learning. As such, we suggest that you spend some time developing a specific improvement plan. To assist you with the initial steps consider the use of the following document. Two activities are set

forth that would be helpful for moving ahead. The target groups and completion timetable show specific entries that must be determined. Think about a few other leadership activities relative to your thoughts about planning and preparing activities and add them to the activity chart.

STEP	YOUR ACTIVITY	TARGET GROUPS / INDIVIDUALS	TARGET COMPLETION DATE
1	Share my concerns relative to gaps in student learning	Department/Grade Level Chairs / School Leadership Team	End of 3rd week of school
2	Decide upon best time and way to include faculty	Department/Grade Level Chairs / School Leadership Team	End of 6th week of school
3			
4			
5			

3. Another decision lies in how and with what individuals or stakeholder groups you will initiate the improvement process. To assist you in making these decisions you could use the grid or table that follows. The list of groups and/or stakeholders that you use should be relevant to your school's situation. In any case, give serious thought to why the individuals or groups are important to be involved in the improvement process.

In the third column of the grid, Point of Contact, identify the point at which the process would be most appropriate for bringing a group into the planning and implementation processes. In the case of department chairs, for example, it might be wise to bring them in at the very outset of the process.

STAKEHOLDER GROUP INDIVIDUAL	REASONS WHY THESE INDIVIDUALS / GROUPS WOULD BE INTERESTED	POINT OF CONTACT
Department Chairs	Teachers, departments and /or grade levels will be impacted most.	Initial stages
Grade-Level Chairs		
Faculty at Large		
Leadership Team		
Central Office Staff		

Source: Adapted from Lezotte & McKee (2002, p. A-5).

REFERENCES

Angelis, J.I., & Wilcox, K.C. (November 2011). Poverty, performance and frog ponds: What best practice research tells us about their connections. *Kappan,* Phi Delta Kappa.

Baldrige Foundation (January 2012). *Learning-centered education—Baldrige education core values.* From: http://www.baldrige21.com/CORE_VALUES/ED/LearningCentered_Education.html.

Collins, J. (2001). *Good to great.* New York: HarperCollins Publishers, Inc.

Glickman, C.D. (1993). *Renewing America's schools.* San Francisco, Calif.: Jossey-Bass Publishers.

Glass, G.V., & Smith, M.L. (1978). *Meta-analysis on research on the relationship of class size and achievement.* San Francisco, Calif.: Far West Laboratory for Educational Research and Development.

Hargrove, R. (1998). *Mastering the art of creative collaboration.* San Francisco, Calif.: McGraw-Hill.

Lezotte, L.W. (1992). *Creating the total quality effective school.* Okemos, Mich.: Effective Schools Products, Ltd.

Lezotte, L.W., & McKee, K.M. (2002). *Assembly required: A continuous school improvement system.* Okemos, Mich.: Effective Schools Products, Ltd.

Lezotte, L.W., & McKee, K.M. (2004). *Implementation guide, Assembly required: A continuous school improvement system.* Okemos, Mich.: Effective Schools Products, Ltd.

Mazzarella, J.A, & Grunty, T. (1989). In S.C. Smith and P.K. Piele (Eds.), *School leadership: Handbook for excellence second edition,* (pp. 9–27). Office of Educational Research and Improvement, Washington, D.C.: OERI contract OERI-R-86-0003.

McCombs, B.L., & Whisler, J.S. (1997). *The learner-centered classroom and school.* San Francisco, Calif.: Jossey-Bass Publishers.

Morgan, G. (1986). *Images of organization.* Newbury Park, Calif.: Sage.

Norton, M.S. (2008). *Human resources administration for educational leaders.* Thousand Oaks, Calif.: Sage.

Norton, M.S., Kelly, L.K., & Battle, A.R. (2012). *The principal as student advocate: Doing what's best for all students.* Larchmont, N.Y.: Eye on Education.

Welch, J., & Byrne, J.A. (2001). *Jack straight from the gut.* New York: Warner Business Books.

Wilcox, K.C., & Angelis, J.I. (2011). *Best practices from high-performing high schools: How successful schools help students stay in school and thrive.* New York: Teachers College Press.

Zenger, J.H., Musselwhite, E., Hurson, K., & Perrin, C. (1994). *Learning teams mastering the new role.* New York: Irwin Professional Publishing.

3

The Development of a School Climate and Culture Learning-Leadership: Creating the Atmosphere for a Learning Environment

In this chapter we ask you to reflect on the learning atmosphere of your school. How do you feel personally about coming to your school each day? Do you truthfully look forward to the relationships that you will have with teachers, students, and other stakeholders of the school community? How do teachers and students feel about working and learning in the school? When people walk onto your campus, what do you believe is their first impression? Do students in the school truly believe that you and the faculty personnel really care about them as individual learners?

To carry out your reflections a step further, we want you to pause and think about, both formally and informally, the atmosphere that exists in your school. On a scale of 1 to 10, for example, how would you assess the school's climate in respect to the social and professional interactions of people? How would you describe the attitudes and behaviors of teachers, students, and community members relative to relationships among faculty, staff, and students of the school? What are the views of students and parents regarding the school's reputation as a learning center?

If you personally hold the belief that your rating of the school's climate is at the higher levels on a 1 to 10 scale, you need to give yourself a pat on the back. However, we plan to challenge you to gain the feeling of others in your school community relative to the questions posed in the foregoing paragraphs. That is, how would your teachers and students rank the school's climate? This chapter will provide many ideas relative to ways that you might utilize to determine the condition of the school's climate from the perspective of other stakeholders.

CHAPTER 3

In this chapter we will explore more fully that atmosphere and examine both the culture and the climate of the school and suggest strategies by which you will be able to maximize these phenomena toward the goal of improved student learning. Our basic premise is that any improvement that you realize in your school's climate will result in a commensurate increase in your students' achievement. The best research on the topic of student achievement supports this contention. "In fact, the quality of the climate appears to be the single most predictive factor in any school's capacity to promote student achievement" (Shindler, Jones, Williams, Taylor, & Cadenas, 2009, p. 1), and that's why this chapter is so important for you to consider.

RESEARCH HAS MADE IT VERY CLEAR: IMPROVING SCHOOL CLIMATE RESULTS IN THE IMPROVEMENT OF STUDENT ACHIEVEMENT

You, as principal, set the tone for the climate of your school. But what other primary benefits are gained by a strong learning culture and healthy school climate besides the important aspect of improved academic performance on the part of your students? We address these benefits in this chapter. We contend that efforts to improve schools and maximize student learning must address and perhaps change educators' thinking about the necessary attitudes and relationships that condition effective student performance.

We begin with a look at the phenomena of school culture and school climate. We focus on the importance of culture and climate relative to the goals and outcomes of the school's programs and activities and how you as principal set the tone for the climate in the school. We emphasize the importance of school culture and climate in enhancing student achievement in your school. What does the research say regarding the influences of school culture and climate on student achievement, staff relations, and the responsibilities of the school principal for improving these phenomena? But first, we ask that you take a few minutes to respond to the true-or-false quiz that follows.

TRUE OR FALSE QUIZ

Directions: Mark each of the following statements as true or false. Avoid simply guessing the answer. In such a case, just leave the response blank.

True or False

____1. The student school climate–student achievement connection has been well established in the research.

____2. In schools where the school climate has been assessed as being low or even "toxic," one can expect that student achievement will be low and students will be classified as underperforming.

CREATING THE ATMOSPHERE FOR A LEARNING ENVIRONMENT

___3. Certain formal interventions or provisions such as the implementation of counselor-student advisory/counseling periods, increasing resources, and other technical means have proven to matter less than educator-student relations concerning the improvement of school climate.

___4. If the process is properly planned and implemented, improving the school's learning culture will happen in a short period of time without conflict.

___5. Unfortunately, even those leaders in effective schools commonly seem to regard the school's learning culture as beyond their control.

___6. A few primary benefits associated with a positive learning climate/culture in the school are fewer suspensions, fewer dropouts, fewer disruptions, less substance abuse, improved discipline, and higher student self-esteem.

___7. When individual school climate ratings are graphed against achievement scores in research studies, the correlation is low at approximately 0.01.

___8. Most every study of school climate reveals the principal's leadership role in the improvement process as being either "insignificant" or "marginal."

___9. Such factors as the school's rituals, performance expectations, artifacts, mission statements, graduation requirements, curriculum focus, and decision-making processes would most likely reflect aspects of the school's culture.

___10. Such practices as bullying definitely detract from the positive aspects of school climate. Yet over 65 percent of bullying happens when adults can't see it.

Quiz Question Answers

The answer to question #1 is **True**. In the volumes of the research literature that presently exist, the conclusion is clear. Climate has a direct and highly influential relationship with the quality of student achievement in the school.

The answer to question #2 is **True**. The literature is replete with both empirical and research evidence that supports the fact that when school climate is improved, a commensurate improvement in school climate is realized. As noted by Norton, 2008; Hoy & Hannum, 1997; and Shindler, et al., 2009, schools with ratings of high academic performance will possess healthy school climates; underperforming schools are likely to have poor climates that are sometimes termed "toxic."

The answer to question #3 is **True**. Studies reveal that " . . . innovations such as advisory periods seem to have a negative correlation with students' academic achievement. This finding suggests that educator-student *relationships* matter more than *formal structures* to improve school climate" (Jones, Yonezawa, Mehan, & McClure, 2008, p. 1).

The answer to question #4 is **False**. On the contrary, the task of implementing the desired learning culture in the school is complex and will only take place over time. Even in those cases when positive planning, in-service, involvement, and communication have taken place, conflicts and disagreements are most likely to occur.

CHAPTER 3

Without such opportunities to question and propose ideas presented, commitment on the part of students, staff, and other stakeholders is unlikely to occur.

The answer to question #5 is **False.** Empirical evidence supports the finding that true learning-leaders accept the responsibility for leading climate and culture change activities in the school. They are open to accepting accountability for results. In regard to the leadership of the school principal, motivation on the part of the principal translates into motivation among students and staff through the function of goals that are "personally valued goals" and central elements of the leader's motivational and commitment structure (Leithwood & Montgomery, 1984, April).

The answer to question #6 is **True.** In addition to improved student academic performance, various studies have reported other school improvements associated with improvements in the school's learning culture. Such improvements include affective dimensions of student behavior such as discipline, relationships, and decrease in dropouts.

The answer to question #7 is **False.** On the contrary, the correlation between the quality of the school's climate and high achievement scores is high; a correlation of 0.7 according to Shindler, et al. (2009).

The answer to question #8 is **False.** Once again, on the contrary, both empirical and pure research results underscore the importance of the school principal's leadership in planning, implementing, and monitoring the activities relative to improvement activities in the area of school climate and culture. In fact, most authorities in the field agree that regardless of the support of the community stakeholders, the school board, and the school staff, without the leadership of the person in the principal's office little progress in school effectiveness will be realized.

The answer to question #9 is **True.** We will discuss this response in detail later in this chapter. Although the topic of culture remains complex and difficult to grasp, individuals who have studied the topic tend to agree that the underlying assumptions relative to "who we are" are portrayed in what the organization believes is important. Such importance is most often revealed in the priorities of the organization, its rituals, what it appears to value, its beliefs about purposes, and similar values.

The answer to question #10 is **True.** Bullying, without question, is a negative behavior that influences school climate. The question posed here, however, serves the purpose of illustrating how bullying and other negative social behaviors other than student achievement influence the condition of the school's climate. The statistic relative to bullying indicates that 65 percent of adults do not see it happening, as reported by Koenig (2012, February) in his article "Culture and Climate at School: Bullying Prevention, Climate and Culture."

A result of 9 or 10 correct answers on the quiz receives a score of Excellent; 7 or 8 is Very Good; 5 or 6 is Good; 3 or 4 is Fair; and below 4 is "you know what." In any case, the topics suggested by the quiz questions will be further developed later in the chapter.

DOES CLIMATE REALLY MATTER?

"After nearly a decade of putting climate on the back burner, a growing number of states are elevating climate back to a front line in the broader effort to improvement and reduce the achievement gap" (Shindler, et al., 2009, p. 1). In fact, a synthesis of research tends to support the Shindler report that suggests that high student achievement scores of students in any school are "virtually impossible" in cases of a school with an unhealthy climate. Furthermore, if a school demonstrates apathy relative to any attempt to improve the climate, the climate most likely will worsen rather than improve.

We contend that success in building a healthy school climate will result in the realization of improved student learning. In a similar vein, the leadership of a school that practices the concept that "failure is not an option" most likely will realize successful student learning; those that are fostering a "failure atmosphere" are likely to witness a reciprocal unsatisfactory academic performance on the part of the student body.

Student performances are far more likely to improve in the affective domain as well as in the academic arena when a positive school climate exists. For example, as we noted previously, student success tends to breed a higher level of self-esteem and improved discipline, better personal relationships, and positive traits of character inside and outside the school.

The terms *school climate* and *school culture* have been examined, defined, and re-defined in the literature throughout the years. In the following section, our purpose is to clarify the similarities and differences of the two terms and explain why climate and culture have become somewhat synonymous in the thinking of most education researchers and practitioners.

CULTURE AND CLIMATE: SIMILAR BUT DIFFERENT

The significance of an organization's culture and climate really is not a contemporary insight. Although the terms *climate* and *culture* were not commonly used in the literature before the 1960s, the well-being of personnel in the organization was emphasized much earlier in such works as Tead and Metcalf's personnel book, *Personnel Administration* (1920). As these authors pointed more than ninety years ago, "If there's harmony in the factory, says the clever motto of the piano factory, there will be harmony in the piano" (p. 7).

When we speak of an individual's personality, most commonly we are thinking about their attitudes about life, their social and professional relationships with people, and their interpersonal behaviors in relation to various life activities. In the same sense, the collective personality of a school sometimes is referred to as the school's *syntality* (Norton, 2008).

Such things as the extent to which school personnel give priority to setting and implementing the school's primary goals and objectives, how the school works to meet the specific interests and needs of students, how the school goes about fostering human relationships, and what the school does to motivate continuous growth and development on the part of students and staff personnel are factors that strongly influence a school's learning climate.

Educators today tend to use the terms *culture* and *climate* interchangeably. This occurrence is due primarily to the fact that, although the two terms are conceptually different, they do have similarities. We speak of the school and its learning culture in relation to such beliefs that all students can learn, each student must be given the opportunity to participate in the various learning opportunities available in the school, individual student interests and needs are of paramount importance relative to student achievement, and the extent to which learning opportunities truly are available for all students in the school.

Indeed, these factors are founded on the values and fundamental beliefs of school community. School culture as well as school climate have links to people, shared goals, environmental factors, attitudes, traditions, and other related factors.

However, school culture is more normative than school climate. Culture encompasses the basic assumptions that the school holds relative to shared beliefs and values that include but go beyond interpersonal relationships. Although internal and external influences can lead to changes in the school's climate over time, changing one's basic assumptions about life and the beliefs and values held by an individual or a group's culture is far more complex (Norton, 2008). For the purposes of this chapter, we place considerable emphasis on school climate as a paramount factor in conditioning the school atmosphere for positive student learning.

Kotter and Heskett (1992) define culture as representing " . . . the behavior patterns or style of the organization that new employees are automatically encouraged to follow by their fellow employees" (p. 4). According to these authors, the more visible aspects of an organization's culture include shared values that are reflected in the goals that the school strives to achieve and the rules that serve to govern the members' behaviors.

Owens (2004) viewed culture from several perspectives. He stated that,

> By organizational culture is meant the *norms* that inform people what is acceptable and what is not, the dominant *values* that the organization cherishes above others, the *basic assumptions* and *beliefs* that are shared by members of the organization, the *'rules'* that must be observed if one is to get along and be accepted as a member, and the *philosophy* that guides the organization in dealing with its employees and its clients. (p. 66)

Perhaps you have witnessed the inculcation of a school's culture upon employees new to the organization. In a typical situation, the new employee learns directly and indirectly "just how things are done around here." The ability to work within the cultural framework of the organization may become very comfortable or very uncomfortable for the individual. In those cases when the individual is uncomfortable with the beliefs and values in place, they often try different ways to change them. They might challenge certain decisions made by the administration or group members. Or they might take a stand and refuse to go along.

When the other members do not support the new member's objections, he or she commonly limits personal interactions with other members and continues to do his or her own thing. The individual is likely to try once again to change the way things are done, but most often has no success. So the individual drifts further away from what the school is attempting to accomplish and ultimately is likely to leave the school.

We include this rather negative picture in this chapter for several reasons. Culture is a strong force within any organization; it is not easily changed. Culture has a strong influence on the climate of the organization; it influences the way members relate and interact. Culture does bring strong beliefs and values to the thinking of the group's members; it determines what is important and if members will or will not commit to it.

The point is that we want to work for a culture that places students and student learning in the forefront of the school's purposes. We want principals to understand that implementing such a culture takes a strong and effective style of leadership. The remaining sections of this chapter center on this needed leadership.

Perhaps Gareth Morgan (1986) said it best: "Managers can influence the evolution of culture by being aware of the symbolic consequences of their actions and by attempting to foster desirable values, but they can never control culture in the sense that many management writers advocate" (p. 139). As one practicing principal told us, "Results from our attempts to institute positive beliefs about values and student learning come slowly and we do not always succeed, but we just keep on trying."

RELATED BENEFITS OF SCHOOL CULTURE IN THE ACCOMPLISHMENT OF STATED SCHOOL PURPOSES

We have emphasized the importance of school climate and culture on the outcomes of student achievement. Several related benefits adapted from the work of Deal and Peterson (1999) are set forth in the following section.

Knowledge of the school's culture:

1. Serves to focus your staff's attention and behavior on what values, goals, and objectives are of paramount importance in the school's mission.
2. Serves as the basis for successful program change and relevant staff improvement efforts.
3. Serves to improve team building and collaborative program activities that result in improved communication, understanding, and problem-solving practices.
4. Provides a bonding of your staff and the school mission that increases the synergy, motivation, and outcomes of ongoing school programs and activities.

5. Builds faculty commitment and improves the relationships among your staff, your students, the administrators, and the members of your school community.
6. Adds to the efficiency and effectiveness of your school's activities and results in improved school and staff productivity.

THE LEADER OF THE FUTURE

The leader of the future needs to be one who actually creates a culture or a value system that is centered on the important factors of courage, humility, and the motivation to constantly learn and grow (Covey, 1996). It is clear that principal leaders of the future will need to know and understand who they are, what they stand for, what their beliefs and values really are, and how these factors loom important in being a leader of learning on the job. Most all authorities agree that the learning culture of your school is driven by the values and norms held by you and your school personnel.

Let's pause for a moment and reflect on the values and norms that you are certain are held by the large majority of your faculty and staff. Figure 3.1 provides a point of departure for your thoughts on this matter. In the left column, four basic ideas about schooling are suggested. Take the necessary time to think about and then list the basic core values and beliefs you hold relative to each entry starting with the words, "I believe . . . ." For example, in regard to teaching, you might enter the core value or belief that teaching must be student-centered. That is, teaching should be based on the real needs and personal interests of each individual student. Or, I believe that teaching should be adjusted to the extent possible on the appropriate learning style of each learner.

Do the same for the entries of learning, students, and school. Don't simply list those values and beliefs that would look good in the eyes of others; rather list what you truly

BASIC FUNCTION	CORE VALUE/BELIEF STATEMENT
TEACHING	1. I believe ...... 2. I believe ......
LEARNING	1. I believe ...... 2. I believe ......
STUDENTS	1. I believe ...... 2. I believe ......
SCHOOL	1. I believe ...... 2. I believe ......
	1. I believe ...... 2. I believe ......
	1. I believe ...... 2. I believe ......
	1. I believe ...... 2. I believe .....
	1. I believe ..... 2. I believe .....

Figure 3.1. Core Values or Basic Beliefs

CREATING THE ATMOSPHERE FOR A LEARNING ENVIRONMENT

believe. Are these the core values and beliefs that you are willing to share with others? Are they the core values and beliefs that you have or are willing to submit for the commitment of the entire faculty and staff?

COMMITMENT TO VALUES AND BELIEFS

We have never met a school principal that did not want to become a better leader toward the goal of becoming a better school. We believe that this journey begins with a soul-searching discussion between you and your faculty and staff concerning what all of you believe about such matters as excellence in teaching, effective learning, a student-centered culture, and the purposes of schooling. As Barth (1990) stated, "What needs to be improved about schools is their culture" (p. 45). That is, everyone in your school needs to be committed to serving students from the set of core values and beliefs determined through deliberate discussions, action research, and implementation of accountable measures of results.

A lack of cultural understanding of the culture most often results in the environment controlling the school leader. Through an understanding of the culture of the school community you are much more able to exert your influence toward meeting the goals established within the school's mission. One school superintendent told us that he believed that the reason more school principals lost their jobs was because they did not truly understand the underlying culture of their school community. He noted that they thought they understood it, but they really never did.

Plamondon (1996) stated the foregoing need in this way: "A successful leader understands that an organization is held together by shared values, beliefs and commitments. That is what enables it to rise above cyclical hardships and gives it tone, fiber, integrity and capacity to endure" (p. 277). This statement serves as the crux of this entire chapter. Its realization does not come easily. It does require your personal soul searching, your personal courage, and your personal commitment to establish a student-centered learning culture.

CONVEYING YOUR FUNDAMENTAL VALUES AND BELIEFS

How might you lead your faculty and staff to arrive at key statements that will convey your school's fundamental beliefs to everyone associated with the school? We share the thoughts of Lezotte and McKee-Snyder (2011) regarding their synthesis of core beliefs held by educators as follows:

- Education is a shared responsibility—Achievement requires commitment and participation of staff, students, family, and community.

- All students can learn—All students have potential that can be developed.
- Rates of learning vary—The time required for mastery has no bearing on the value of the learner.
- All students have unique skills and talents—Individual abilities must be identified and nurtured.
- High self-esteem enhances success—People develop best through sincere praise and validation. (p. 70)

We ask that you read once again the foregoing core beliefs. Do these beliefs coincide with your personal values and beliefs? We challenge you to stop and give thought to the third core belief in the foregoing listing. What does this belief really imply relative to how we value students? Current practices relating to student failure and retention in grade? How we group, test, and evaluate student performance? How we use students' learning styles? What other questions might the entry raise in your mind?

CORE VALUES GUIDING YOUR SCHOOL

In order to take the suggestions in the foregoing section to the next level, you might set aside a professional development day to complete the suggested exercise with your entire faculty and staff. If you choose to do so, begin the process of arriving at or confirming a set of core values and beliefs for the school. Patience is a necessary virtue in such an effort; it might take several attempts before you and the staff will be prepared to commit to what you truly believe about such important matters as teaching, learning, student-centered concepts, and purposes of schooling.

One school principal pointed out that the term *excellence* popped up in their discussions quite often. He asked each teacher to take the time to write out their definition of the term and to hand in their concept of the term within one week. The principal printed the teachers' concepts of excellence on a sheet of paper and distributed them at the next school improvement meeting. Members began to discuss the "definitions" immediately. How were the definitions similar or different? Which were especially insightful? Which definitions did they tend to accept? As a result of this brief discussion, a mutual concept of the term *excellence* came into being.

Over time and once you have formulated your school's beliefs about such responsibilities as teaching, student learning, excellence, and school purposes, we recommend that you move toward establishing a set of core values to which every person commits. Here is a word of caution. Keep in mind that beliefs, values, and basic assumptions about what is important in life are more difficult to agree upon and change than certain attitudes and norms of behavior.

Most authorities point out that a set of core values and meaningful relevant purposes are of paramount importance in building what commonly we refer to as a vision for the school. We assume that your vision will lead to the realization that schools consist of opportunities for all students to learn according to their individual potential, their personal needs, and interests.

We submit that when this vision is accomplished, you will consider it to be the important feature of your legacy as a school leader. You will be proud of the results of your leadership that led the school to implement beliefs and values that centered on the ultimate success of learning for all students in the school.

EXAMPLES OF VALUE STATEMENTS AND CULTURAL NORMS

As emphasized in the foregoing section, values and beliefs constitute the core ingredients of a school's learning culture. Likewise, the culture of your school is directly impacted by the values and beliefs that are ultimately developed, internalized, and incorporated into every decision made and every action taken by every employee in the school. A consideration of school values and beliefs from a learning-leader's point of view must be taken very seriously.

The mission statement that "Our culturally diverse population is viewed as a strength; a spirit of equity, cooperation, and respect permeates our school community; and our community reflects a number of values embraced by the school and school district" speaks loudly for the importance of the students, cooperative and collaborative programming and decision making, the commitment to student diversity, and equity for students from diverse populations and those with special needs.

During one interview session conducted as part of the planning for this book, we noticed mission statements posted in several prominent places in the school. One was placed near the main entrance to the school. Another was placed on the wall of the school's office. One appeared on the principal's office wall. Another was seen near the main bulletin board in the central corridor of the school.

As we toured the school and met briefly with school faculty personnel, support staff members, and a few individual students, we asked as diplomatically as possible if the school had a mission statement or something that underscored the main purposes of the school. Although the large majority of the persons that were approached answered "yes," none could relate the mission statement's primary focus. Don't let this happen to you.

THE UTILIZATION OF A CULTURAL NORMS SURVEY

The values and beliefs held by the school constitute a school's cultural norms. The extent to which the faculty and staff commit to and implement these norms contributes significantly to the long-term outcomes of improvement efforts. A helpful way to assess the extent to which your school faculty and staff are committed to various value/belief statements is to use a cultural norm survey such as that developed by Lezotte and McKee-Snyder (2011). Of course, you could use your own list of values and beliefs that have resulted from your previous efforts. Gaining faculty and community commitment to values/beliefs in this process does take both patience and time.

At a school program improvement session, meet with a representative group or entire faculty membership to discuss the value norms. In the case of the norms shown in figure 3.2, determine if they suggest and/or reflect the norms of your school. Take the liberty in changing or adding any norms that are applicable to your situation. You might want to add a further description to some of the entries in figure 3.2. For example, for item 1, High Expectations, you might add "High Expectations *for Student Achievement*."

Ask each member in attendance to check the appropriate level in the figure that reflects the current status of the norms in your school. Collect the members' responses and take time later to analyze the results. As you consider the members' assessments of the stated norms, you will be able to identify those areas of the school's culture that are on the weak or strong side. You will be able to determine the extent of differences of opinion, if any, concerning each norm item. In some cases, you will be able to ascertain the effectiveness of previous efforts that might have been implemented. And of major importance, you will have motivated the thinking of the participants relative to the questions of the school's purposes, values, and beliefs. You most likely have set the stage for additional thinking about who we are and whom we serve.

ITEM	DESCRIPTION	VERY WEAK	WEAK	NEUTRAL	STRONG	VERY STRONG
1	Collegiality					
2	Openness to Experimentation					
3	High Expectations					
4	Trust or Confidence					
5	Tangible Support					
6	Expanding Knowledge Base of Teaching and Learning					
7	Appreciation and Recognition					
8	Caring, Celebration and Humor					
9	Involvement in Decision Making					
10	Maintenance of Traditions					
11	Protection of Important Matters					
12	Honest and Open Communications					

Figure 3.2. Cultural Norms Survey
Source: Lezotte & McKee (2004). Implementation guide, Assembly required: A continuous school improvement system. (p. 35).

Assume that the respondents recorded a strong level of response for high expectations but also recorded a weak level of response for trust and confidence. As principal, what might you determine as the implications of those perceptions? Would such a response tend to make you look inwardly at your own behavior patterns? Might such responses encourage you to take them back to the participants or an appropriate leadership team for further discussion and honest feedback? Results from the norms assessment can serve to foster important actions. They most likely will give you an opportunity to celebrate, but certainly will provide data that can direct your efforts toward improvement in the school's culture.

WHAT YOU SHOULD KNOW ABOUT SCHOOL CLIMATE

We previously contended that one of the most direct ways that the school principal can improve student achievement in the school is to make every effort to improve the school's climate. We also believe that those schools that are excelling and/or rated as A or A+ schools would score highly on any measure that might be used to determine its climate status. On the other hand, those schools that are assessed as underperforming schools will find such climate measures to be far less positive.

The attitude that "you either you have it or don't have it" regarding positive climate is unsatisfactory.

Both pure and empirical research support the fact that the climate in any school can be improved (Lunenburg & Ornstein, 2004; Parades & Frazer, 1992; Hopkins & Crain, 1985; Rutherford, 1985; Sweeney, 1992; Hoy & Hannum, 1997; Norton, 2008; and Shindler, et al., 2009). We focus on this topic later in the chapter.

How School Climate Is Defined

Pause and take just a moment to write out your own one- or two-sentence definition of school climate. What specific adjectives, factors, or behaviors did your definition include? You will have no difficulty finding definitions of the term *organization* or *school climate* in the literature. Norton (2008) defined climate as " . . . the collective personality of a school or school system. It is the atmosphere that prevails as characterized by the social and professional interactions of people" (p. 237).

The National School Climate Center (2012) defined climate as " . . . the quality and character of school life as it relates to norms and values, interpersonal relations and social interactions, and organizational processes and structures" (p. 1). Within the parameters of this definition are such characteristics as the establishment of clear school goals; high expectations for student learning including a variety of opportunities for students to learn; a high level of interpersonal relations among the school personnel, students, and parents; cooperative work efforts; open communication systems accompanied by high evidence of trust; a caring school leader evidenced by his or her activities as a student advocate; and the existence of high esprit within the school community. For the purposes of this chapter, the foregoing climate definition set forth by Norton (2008) will suffice.

There are other ways that we can look at climate and its characteristics. Some authorities attempt to describe it in terms of the status of the physical, social, affective, and academic environments. For example, overcrowdedness in the school, poor condition of school facilities, unkempt school grounds and inside facilities, and outdated instructional resources influence the school climate adversely. In the area of the social environment, poor teacher-student, teacher-parent, and parent-administrator relations project an unhealthy school climate situation.

Certain practices implemented by the school faculty and staff such as discipline procedures also affect the school's climate positively or negatively. If administrators and teachers hold the view that the only thing that students understand is punishment, negative social relationships are certain to prevail. Such views attribute to what is termed a *toxic climate*. On the other hand, if the administration and staff discipline as an opportunity for the student to learn and invoke what is termed *nonpunitive discipline*, then climate conditions tend to improve. That is, discipline becomes a learning process and is implemented in the best interests of the student.

The point in the foregoing discussion is that "The culture and climate of the school can be affected by factors from disciplinary problems and classroom rowdiness to educator pessimism or student apathy. Culture and climate . . . can most nearly be described as the sum of all perceptions and emotions attached to the school, both good and bad, held by students, faculty, administrators, parents, and the community at large" (e-Lead, 2012, p. 1).

The Determinants of School Climate

The importance of school climate certainly is not a new topic in the professional education field. Nearly forty years ago a group of school principals, superintendents, professors, and educational directors met under the sponsorship of Phi Delta Kappa to consider the recommendations of some 200 school administrators involved in school climate endeavors. The result of the group's efforts was the publication *School Climate Improvement: A Challenge to the School Administrator* (1973). In our opinion, this publication remains a hallmark for its contribution to the importance of school climate toward the goal of improving student achievement.

It is beyond our purpose of this chapter to present the many significant concepts and administrative wisdom set forth in Phi Delta Kappa's publication. However, the following section emphasizes the primary concepts set forth by the study group relative to various indicators of school climate and how these indicators are inextricably tied to student learning. The following information is based upon information in the aforementioned Phi Delta Kappa publication. School climate descriptions and specific indicators were a result of input from school staffs and administrators who were presently working on school climate improvement programs (Phi Delta Kappa, 1973). Three specific climate determinants were identified: *Program Determinants, Process Determinants,* and *Material Determinants* (see figure 3.3).

School Climate Program Determinants

Program determinants include those opportunities provided by the school's leadership for enhancing the learning process for all students. Learning experiences are relevant in that they not only are in the best interests of each individual learner, but they result in the student's ability to implement their learning knowledge and skills. Figure 3.3 sets forth several components of program determinants.

For example, the school program offers many opportunities for active learning; students become totally involved in the learning process. School programs and experiences are individualized in the sense that the personal needs and interests of the student loom important. Performance expectations are based on the present status of the learner and are initiated at the success level of the individual student as opposed to a group expectation.

In addition, varied learning environments are planned for the learner including both in-class and out-of-class activities. Extracurricular activities are viewed as important learning opportunities. Each student has a role in determining his or her own program needs. In many instances, community resources, both human and material, are utilized to foster varied learning opportunities for students.

The principal, teachers, students, staff, and parents are actively involved in determining and fulfilling program determinants. For example, the school principal provides ongoing evaluation and feedback regarding opportunities for student learning. Students regularly interact with teachers and others to determine individual learning activities. Staff personnel are supportive in providing active learning opportunities (e.g., counselors, nurses, librarians, and physical/sports staff). Parents are well informed regarding how they can support active learning experiences in the home.

School Climate Process Determinants

Process determinants center on the school's structures and procedures for identifying and dealing with the existence of problems through problem solving, initiating effective procedures, and assessing their results. That is, a school with effective process determinant components is able to initiate problem-solving skills that resolve problems and conflicts with minimal energy.

As noted in figure 3.3, effective communication, conflict resolution, participative decision making, acceptance of accountability for student progress, and effective instructional strategies are among the various determinants that affect school climate. Each

CLIMATE FACTORS AND TARGET AREAS FOR IMPROVEMENT

PROGRAM DETERMINANTS
↓

Opportunities for Active Learning
Individualized Performance Expectations
Varied Learning Environments
Flexible Curriculum and Extracurricular Activities
Support and Structure Appropriate to Learner's Maturity
Rules Cooperatively Determined
Varied Reward Systems

PROCESS DETERMINANTS
↓

Problem Solving Ability
Development of School Goals
Identifying and Working with Conflicts
Effective Communications
Involvement in Decision Making
Autonomy with Accountability
Effective Teaching-Learning Strategies
Ability to Plan for the Future

MATERIAL DETERMINANTS
↓

Adequate Resources
Supportive and Efficient Logistical System
Suitability of School Plant

↓

IMPROVED SCHOOL CLIMATE

Figure 3.3. The School Climate Profile: Program, Process, and Material Determinants
Source: Phi Delta Kappa, School Climate Improvement: A Challenge to the School Administrator (1973). Robert S. Fox, et al. Reprinted by permission.

member of your school and school community must work cooperatively to identify and define problems or weakness in the school's programs and procedures. For example, consider your role and the roles of teachers, staff, students, and parents in the continuous improvement of school goals. The primary purpose of goal improvement is to help all school stakeholders understand the important reasons that your school exists.

As school principal, one way that you can contribute to the process determinants is to develop key reference points (mission, school goals and objectives, school rules, school community resources, award systems, etc.). Teachers can take personal responsibility for their own professional growth needs. Students can assume a major responsibility for their own learning. They can take seriously the opportunity to develop personal learning goals that center on their own special needs, interests, and abilities. Staff personnel can work to schedule time to assist students by advocating for their personal rights as learners. Parents must assume their primary responsibility for supporting the learning program and its objectives for their child by not violating at home what the school is attempting to achieve for their child.

School Climate Material Determinants

Material determinants are those resources that are needed by the school and its members to foster the environment and support the learning program for each student in the school. This determinant includes the allocation of adequate resources, the implementation of a supportive and efficient system for securing quality school personnel, providing the necessary instructional resources needed for effective teaching and student learning, and providing important school services (e.g., secretarial services, counseling, student scheduling, custodial services, business requirements, and others).

The national economy and ongoing educational budget cuts make the foregoing considerations "just easy to say." Empirical evidence in schools today reveals that obtaining adequate resources for a quality learning program is problematic; teachers often are paying for instructional materials that they need in the classroom; parents are being "forced" to pay for instructional materials and many program activities in order for their child to participate; and parents and community members are encouraged to donate funds to the school and take a tax deduction. The monetary costs for needed school repairs and construction of new schools have become one of the major, serious problems for American schools. Student safety in many school situations is a concern of paramount importance.

We submit that the school principal can serve a good purpose in this process by establishing expectations on the part of the custodial staff, students, and other school personnel to keep the school environment as attractive as possible. All persons can serve to keep the school's internal and external spaces attractive by emphasizing the importance of adding and not detracting from the "beauty" of their school; students are responsible for helping to see that their school is kept clean and in good repair. The exhibiting of student work in appropriate places in the school or outside landscaping might be a project for the student council or other student group.

In any case, the school principal must develop a plan for purchasing school resources on a priority basis. Teachers become instrumental in any such effort. We suggest that teachers in specific grades and/or specific subjects develop a materials purchasing priority plan. That is, the first priority should require that each teacher work toward the obtaining of materials that have been determined as *essential resources* for that grade or subject.

The next priority is that of *highly desirable* resource materials; the third priority is *enrichment resources.* Rather than allocate each teacher a certain amount of funds each year to purchase resources, the essential resources are first made available to teachers who do not have them in the classroom. When all classrooms have the essential resources, then the highly desirable resources are purchased as appropriate to the budget.

Instruments for assessing school climate also are quite prevalent. One such climate instrument, the School Climate Assessment Instrument (SCAI) developed by the Alliance for the Study of School Climate (ASSC), includes several specific dimensions for the construct of climate (e.g., faculty relations, student interactions, discipline environment, school-community relations, and others). The SCAI and other assessment instruments for measuring your school's climate will be discussed later in the chapter.

School Climate: How It Can Be Measured

Jonathan Cohen (2007, Fall) reported on one school leader's views of climate evaluations as follows:

> I used school climate findings as a faculty development tool to help faculty know what we are doing well and what we need to do differently. We discussed it at several meetings. We brainstormed together—what are all the things we can do to improve? I used it as tangible evidence, not just my opinion. I used it in work with new teachers and discussed the implications with the board of trustees. I have discussed it with students in the communication and socialization classes. I am using it to plan a manual . . . listing the 10 ways we might address a given item that emerged in the (Comprehensive School Climate Inventory) in the curriculum. We want it to help us set goals and inform our practice for the long run (p. 6).

Interestingly enough, the overwhelming majority of learning-leaders believe that school climate matters and that school climate should be measured. We asked one principal interviewee the question, "How do you evaluate the school's climate?" He responded, "Well, I listen a lot." Indeed listening isn't a bad idea, but there are a variety of ways that you can evaluate your school's climate. For example, the establishment of a focus group to carry out a series of interviews with community representatives, teacher groups, student organizations, and parent associations can result in gaining information from a variety of school stakeholders.

In the following section, we will discuss several sources that provide valid and reliable instruments for measuring school climate. In addition, we do not hesitate to recommend less formal instruments that can be used to gain climate feedback from teachers, students, parents, and other community members. Although we encourage you to implement some beneficial method for measuring your school's climate, we want to underscore the importance of using the results for improvement purposes. Just your assumption of leadership of the implementation of a school climate survey and having an open discussion of its results will give your faculty, students, and parents an appreciation for the fact that "your concern for improvement is showing."

Examples of Climate Assessment Instruments

Cost factors tend to prohibit the utilization of commercial climate instruments. However, such instruments provide a method for ensuring valid and reliable assessment results. In addition, most commercial assessment instruments save the school's time of having to score and analyze the climate survey results. In most cases, the comprehensive data resulting from commercial instruments provide comparative state and national norms with the norms achieved by your school's assessment results.

A few of the climate instruments that have been widely used nationally include the following:

The OCDQ (Organizational Climate Description Questionnaire) by Halpin and Croft (1962) is the "grandfather" of climate assessment instruments. It has been revised several times by other authorities and altered for uses at the various levels of school organization. In general, the OCDQ instruments use four areas to describe a school's climate: open, engaged, disengaged, and closed.

The CFK School Climate Profile (Phi Delta Kappa, 1973) is designed so that a variety of individuals can complete the survey. It focuses on the three climate determinants that were previously discussed in this chapter.

The Organizational Health Inventory (OHI-S) serves to assess seven climate areas including principal influence, morale, academic emphasis, and others. The instrument was developed by Hoy and others in 1991.

The High School Characteristics Index (HSCI), although developed in 1964 by G.G. Stern, has been one of the most popular assessment instruments for measuring school climate. The HSCI includes thirty climate scales that relate to seven factors of school climate such as achievement standards, personal dignity, and others.

The Purdue Teacher Opinionaire (PTO) developed by Bentley and Rempel in 1964 focuses on the assessment of teacher morale. Such climate factors as teacher load, rapport among teachers, teacher and administrator rapport, and community support of education are included in the assessment.

The Comprehensive School Climate Inventory (CSCI) is used to assess five major areas of school climate: safety, teaching, learning, relationships, and the environment.

The research-based assessment instrument was designed by Center for Social and Emotional Education.

The Hope Survey enables schools to assess their school environment through the eyes of students by measuring perceptions of autonomy, belongingness, goal orientation, as well as engagement in learning and dispositions toward achievement. More about the Hope Survey can be obtained on the Web.

The School Culture Triage Survey serves to quickly and accurately determine a school's culture. The survey was developed by G. Phillips in 1996 and later revised and redesigned by others. The instrument focuses on the school's culture. However, climate factors such as the student's perception of belongingness and hope are included as well as climate factors that center on the school's environmental conditions.

The Comprehensive Assessment of School Environment (CASE, 1987): **School Climate Surveys** (National Association of Secondary School Principals). These school climate surveys are among the most commonly used assessment instruments used by schools nationally. The surveys are adjustable for relevant use by parents, students, or teachers. Such factors as student academic orientation, teacher-student relationships, student-peer relationships, and instructional management are included in the survey's coverage.

Of course, many more climate assessment instruments are available to schools. Empirical evidence suggests that many schools and school districts develop their own climate assessment instruments. One of the advantages of this kind of instrument is vested in the fact that it most likely focuses on the climate factors that are most relevant to the school's concerns. Thus content validity of the instrument can be high. One of its drawbacks is the fact that it does not have other state or national norms for comparison purposes.

The School Can Develop Its Own Climate Assessment Instrument

The following figure 3.4 is an example of a locally developed school climate instrument. The Wymore School Climate Instrument was designed by members of a climate improvement team for use by any local school or school district. It is directed primarily to the parents of the school district.

As noted in figure 3.4, four climate areas are included in the survey instrument. For each major climate area, several climate descriptors are indicated. For example, for the major area of Home-School Relations, the assessment descriptors include such descriptors as parental communications with the school, parental requests and the school's responses, and the parents' perceptions of their child's view of the school. Each descriptor is rated on a Likert scale from 1, Never occurs, to 5, Always occurs.

Our intention here is not only to suggest the use of such locally developed climate assessment instruments, but to encourage you to work with your staff to design an appropriate assessment tool that fits the interests and needs particularly appropriate for your situation.

Directions: Use the following scale to assess parents' perceptions of each of the entries on the climate assessment scale: 5—Always occurs, 4—Frequently occurs, 3—Sometimes occurs, 2—Seldom occurs, 1—Never occurs. Please use the enclosed self-addressed, stamped envelope to return the questionnaire. **Circle the rating that applies in each case.**

1	**Home-School Relations**					
a	Parental communications with faculty and staff personnel at Wymore Elementary School are positive.	1	2	3	4	5
b	My child/children have good things to say about Wymore Elementary School's faculty and staff.	1	2	3	4	5
c	My requests and/or concerns regarding Wymore School matters are handled promptly and courteously.	1	2	3	4	5
d	My child's/children's teacher(s) communicate with me appropriately regarding matters of academic progress, behavior, or other matters of parental concern.	1	2	3	4	5
2	**School Curriculum, Programs, and Activities**					
a	The Wymore Elementary School administration and faculty keep me well informed relative to developments in the school's curriculum, programs, and activities.	1	2	3	4	5
b	Opportunities for parents to participate in school curricular developments and other student program activities at Wymore School are readily available to parents.	1	2	3	4	5
c	Parents' conferences are well planned and relevant to parental interests.	1	2	3	4	5
d	School programs and activities for parents at Wymore Elementary School are relevant and worthwhile.	1	2	3	4	5
3	**The Environment of the Wymore Elementary School**					
a	The behavior of Wymore students in the school building and on the school campus is positive.	1	2	3	4	5
b	My child/children are well treated by other Wymore Elementary School children.	1	2	3	4	5
c	When I visit the school or observe students on the school campus, student behavior and courtesy are positive.	1	2	3	4	5
d	The Wymore Elementary School is a friendly place.	1	2	3	4	5
4	**Observations and Comments** **(Please respond briefly to each of the following questions relative to the Wymore Elementary School and Its Environment.)**					
1	What suggestions do you have that would lead to improvements and a better atmosphere at the Wymore Elementary School?					
2	How would you describe the strengths of Wymore Elementary School's program and atmosphere for student learning? For example, think about its strengths in relation to curriculum, communication effectiveness, achievement, school-parental relationships, etc.					

Figure 3.4. Example of a Locally Developed Climate Assessment

CHAPTER 3

THE TASK OF IMPROVING THE CULTURE AND CLIMATE OF YOUR SCHOOL

The tasks and challenges involved in improving the culture and climate of your school are such that you first must purchase a magic wand. Although we are not able to list specific resources for a purchase, sometimes we gain the ideas that they are available from such sources as the school critics, state legislatures, and authors of books on education that seem to have all the answers. We regret that you have to work without the benefits of a magic wand, but we do have some recommendations as to how you might proceed and/or continue your efforts to do your best to establish a learning climate in your school.

As your commitment to your role as learning-leader at your school, most likely you have asked yourself what must be done to initiate programs and behaviors that support commitment and result in improvements in student learning. Your decision relative to initiating and/or continuing your efforts in this regard depends largely on your personal leadership style.

You might take the approach used by one of the principals that we interviewed. He told us that at the very outset of his tenure in a new principal's position, he informed the staff that he believed in the student benefits of an inclusive school. It took him the first three years to prove to his faculty and parents of the school that inclusiveness was in the best interests of all students in the school. Nevertheless, within that time period, the faculty and staff were able to witness the benefits of inclusiveness, and their commitment to it was evidenced.

On the other hand, your style might suggest a more subtle approach. You might begin by asking questions about what faculty members think about inclusiveness, student-centered program activities, or student advocacy. For example, you might read a page from one of the contentions in this chapter and ask your teachers or a group of parents, "What do you think about the belief that all students can learn?" Or "A book that I am reading says that 'School culture and climate are primary factors in the improvement of student achievement in schools.' What are your thoughts about this?" You most likely will be surprised with the interest that your question generates.

COLLABORATION IN A CONTINUOUS LEARNING CYCLE

Consider the Agua Fria Union High School District in Arizona, where a continuous leaning cycle has been implemented in its schools. Using the cycle shown in figure 3.5, teachers assemble by discipline such as mathematics, science, and language arts and complete the steps as noted.

A common activity chart, figure 3.6, for reporting team activities for the specific disciplines can be quite helpful for the school principal. For example, knowing what

CREATING THE ATMOSPHERE FOR A LEARNING ENVIRONMENT

STEP	ACTIVITY
1	Teachers collect and analyze end of unit/quarter/semester student performance data.
2	Teachers identify standards in which student performance was the lowest or the standard not met.
3	Teachers generate a goal toward which student performance will improve to meet the standard.
4	Teachers generate interventions and formative assessments addressing not-met standards.
5	Teachers implement the instructional strategy or intervention.
6	Teachers administer end-of-intervention or strategy assessment.
7	Teachers identify which interventions were successful and which interventions were unsuccessful.
8	Teachers retain successful interventions and modify or discard unsuccessful interventions.
9	Teachers analyze student performance and move students on to new material or additional remediation.

Figure 3.5. Data-Driven Processes to Improve Student Learning
Source: Adapted from Agua Fria Union High School District, Curriculum Division, 2012. Printed with permission.

specific committee activities are in progress and which team members have assumed the responsibility for each one enables the principal to keep abreast of team meeting activities, team progress, and team accomplishments.

Although the improvement process is cyclical, the process theoretically begins with collection of performance data from a variety of state and local school sources. This step is closely tied to the information of standard core requirements that might be determined by the state and is likely to include the requirements of the local school board as well. The process continues through evaluation activities relative to the curriculum presently in place. Specific activities by teachers are briefly described in the data-driven-decision-making table.

XYZ High School

Committee / Team: __School Climate Committee__

School Goal / Project: __Achieve a score of 4.5 on the School Climate Survey__

Committee/Team Members: _Faculty: A. Jones, M. Brown, B. Smith, S. White Students: R. Williams, L. Scott_

TASK	DESCRIPTION	RESPONSIBLE	DUE DATE
1	Administer the school climate survey to all students & faculty	Jones & White	9/15
2	Collect surveys and compile scores	Jones & White	9/30
3	Disaggregate student scores by gender, ethnicity & grade level	Committee	10/30
4	Identify areas of strength and areas needing improvement	Committee	11/15
5	Report findings to faculty and to student leadership groups	Brown / Scott	
6			
7			
8			

Figure 3.6. Committee/Team Log

CHAPTER 3

IMPROVEMENT IDEAS THAT YOU CAN IMPLEMENT IMMEDIATELY

You can do many things almost immediately to generate interest in learning improvement on the part of your staff and students. We summarize several such strategies and activities in the following section. You will be able to add your own ideas and those ideas that already have been initiated by others on the staff.

Incentive Sites in the School

One of the first and easiest strategies that you might consider to improve school climate is to create what we call incentive, pride, or accomplishment sites around your campus. A variety of examples of student, staff, and school accomplishments is displayed. Think about all of the areas in which you are seeking improvement: improved attendance, fewer tardies, no graffiti, a cleaner campus, improved relationships, improvements in academic achievements, and others. Recognizing positive behaviors on the part of students may lead to a student of the week or a group accomplishment of the month.

Potential incentive sites abound inside and outside the school. What kinds of material are displayed on the bulletin boards? What kinds of information can be seen in the faculty lounge? How are important student achievements revealed? What impressions does one get when entering the restrooms? Does the entrance to the school suggest a friendly atmosphere and the important purposes of the school? Begin by soliciting input from all persons in the school. Make certain that they understand that you want to hear every idea for an incentive site in the school and that each idea will be given consideration.

The Idea Board or Suggestion Box

One principal implemented the concept of an idea board or suggestion box whereby any staff member or student could write an idea or suggestion on a 3 x 5 index card and post it on the idea board or place it in the suggestion box. The idea could be on an anonymous basis or signed as desired. The cards were gathered on a regular basis, usually weekly or biweekly, and reviewed by an appropriate group or committee. One way to gather the important ideas from students and/or teachers is to ask them.

Similar to what is reported on one contemporary TV pawn shop program, "One never knows what might come through the door." In one instance, a high school student wrote a complaint about the lack of student involvement in the decision-making process concerning student regulations. He signed his name. As a result, conversations about student rights and student participation in matters concerning them were initiated. Ultimately the student council was reimplemented in the school.

The Data Board

Robinson and Buntrock (2011) identified a school that created a data wall that tracked movement in student achievement. The school staff held meetings to interpret the data, and the building leadership used the data to inform teachers and others; results were used to modify instruction. The same principal who created the data wall also created places where students could post their best academic work. She called these locations "jewel boxes" that served as incentives to motivate improved student success.

A Hall of Fame Photo Gallery

The hallway leading from the entrance of the school building into the gymnasium in one high school in Chandler, Arizona, features photos of students and teams who have excelled in academics, athletics, and the arts. The photos include the name of the student or team, the specific accomplishment, and other information, including the year of the accomplishment. How about the possibility of a hall of fame for other school programs including reading, science, music, social studies, industrial arts, English and English composition, and others?

Posting Scholarships and Special Academic Awards Earned by Students

Some schools post such things as the dollar value earned by graduating seniors on posters in the form of a thermometer in appropriate places in the hallways of the school. Students, teachers, and parents who walk by the poster take pride in the accomplishments shown on the poster. The posting of the monetary results of scholarship awards earned by students serves as an incentive on the part of other students for grade improvements that might qualify them for such awards later in their school years.

Learning Snapshot #1—The principal of Tarwater Elementary School, Chandler, Arizona, stated that "he wants his school to be the centerpiece of community pride." He wanted the school to be seen as a place where parents feel welcome and are proud of the fact that their children attend his school. He achieved this goal in part by telling parents that being involved with their children's education is a nonnegotiable item.

He initiated a wide variety of opportunities for parents to get "plugged in" to their child's program; parents were viewed as partners in their child's education. Such family events as the Fall Festival Curriculum Night, the Family Spring BBQ, the Art Masterpiece Gallery, school concerts, and student performances provide opportunities for parents to participate throughout the school year.

The school running club has various events in which parents are invited to participate. Parents are invited to join in the school's unique "mousetrap" car races. Parents are encouraged and often seen having lunch with their children at the school.

CHAPTER 3

Best Practices for Improving the School's Climate: What the Research Says

We analyzed and then synthesized approximately 250 professional articles, textbook chapters, research papers, interviews, and notes from lectures and presentations on the topics of organizational management, educational leadership, and school climate and culture. The results of this synthesis are reported in the following section. The primary guide for the examination of these findings centered on the question "What administrative behaviors, environmental conditions, strategies, and program provisions are most commonly reported in relation to fostering healthy climates in organizations including schools and school districts?" The factors most commonly reported in the synthesis are as follows:

1. Meaningful goals and objectives that have been developed for the organization. Whether they are termed *goals, purposes, objectives, ends, aims, mission,* or other such terms, the development of a set of shared goals was the most commonly named feature related to organizations with open and healthy climates. This feature also was stipulated more than seventy years ago by Barnard (1938) when he underscored the three major functions of any organization: purpose, communication, and commitment.

> Educational goals stem from the culture of a social system. Goals are statements that express the aims of education and provide guiding purposes that it should strive to achieve. The beliefs, values, ethics, and basic assumptions upon which a social system is founded set the bases for the guiding goals that the system's many institutions are established to achieve.
>
> (Norton, 2005, p. 189)

We have emphasized the point that goals and mission must be collaboratively developed in order that personal commitment is achieved on the part of all parties. That is, mission statements and goals that have not been internalized in terms of the specific values and beliefs in the school community are unlikely to become successfully operational in the school's program activities.

Wynne (1981) examined 140 schools for the purpose of differentiating effective and ineffective schools. He used the term *coherence* to underscore the most important feature of effective schools, the integration of several elements in the school. One such element is the need for all stakeholders to understand the mission of the school, its goals and expectations for student performance. Another element relates to the factors of goal direction, equality of staff treatment, and staff cooperation. Each of these factors relates closely to the climate condition of the school.

2. The Development of a Viable Self-Image and High Performance Expectations

Research by Edmonds (1982), Cuban (1998), Ornstein & Levine (2003), and other authorities has emphasized the characteristics of "high expectations" relative to student and staff performance in the accomplishment of an effective school. "Money does not seem to be the key or secret ingredient; rather, a number of intangible items that promote school effectiveness and productivity seem to coincide with school climate or culture" (Lunenburg & Ornstein, 2004, p. 409).

Effective schools have a clear idea of "who they are" and "where they are going." Effective schools are inclusive schools in the sense that each child, regardless of personal ability, is prized for the contributions he or she can make to the accomplishment of school purposes. Such a philosophy is one pillar that forms the foundation of a school's viable self-image and an open positive school climate. In every case, it is expected that each individual will work to achieve his or her full potential.

In relation to self-image and high expectations, Edmonds (1982), Purkey and Smith (1983), and Stedman (1987) found sets of factors common to effective schools. In all three sets of factors, high expectations, orderly climates, and the principal's instructional leadership were named as being of paramount importance for creating the foundation for school effectiveness.

3. Opportunities for Self-Development and Personal Growth

Your school will grow and develop as the people in the school progress. In this sense, schools are people, and this truth underscores the concepts of McGregor (1960) and others who studied human motivation relative to the potential of people and their inner desire to become better administrators, better teachers, and better support personnel. Findings that support the importance of growth opportunities for organizations are revealed in numerous studies. In short, the single most significant factor driving job satisfaction is the opportunity for growth and career development (Bathhurst, 2007).

Staff development is not something that organizations "do to employees," rather its effectiveness depends on the extent to which it is personalized and centered on the special interests and needs of each individual. In many respects, personal growth is self-development. Forced growth, if effective at all, is likely to be short lived. Motivated learning-leaders assume the primary responsibility for their own professional development. Your role as principal in this regard is to assess the development needs and interests of school personnel and open the doors of opportunity for individual growth to take place.

A rapidly developing term in the area of organizational administration is that of *talent management*. Talent management is based on the concept that organizations and workers are most productive when emphasis is placed on talents and strengths as opposed to concentrating on improving weaknesses. As discussed in depth in

Clifton and Nelson's book (1992) *Soar with Your Strengths*, when individuals are able to contribute to the system in areas where their primary interests and strengths prevail, major improvements in job satisfaction, personal motivation, and organizational productivity result. The healthy school makes special efforts to identify the strengths of school personnel and their placement in roles where their talents can be exercised.

The implications for your work as school principal are summarized as follows. You must assume a leadership role in the process of staff development for all personnel, but this role focuses more on assessing school and staff interests and needs and providing multiple opportunities for the staff to meet growth needs. The underlying focus is self-development that is welcomed by professional personnel in a school with a student learning environment.

4. Initiator, Contributor, Disseminator, and User of a Viable Set of School and School System Policies, Regulations, and Rules

The legal world of the school principal and the importance of viable school district policies and administrative regulations loom important when it comes to the implementation of a student-centered learning school. However, the importance of factor #4 rests in the fact that clear school district policies, administrative regulations, and local school rules are of vital importance to fostering a positive climate in the school. Such policies, regulations, and rules influence your school's climate in a variety of ways.

(1) Effective policies and regulations are the primary vehicles that give guidance to what your school is to accomplish but also provide for the implementation of your discretion. Policies are the primary vehicle for establishing the important goals that a school district and school are to achieve.

As noted previously, viable goals are of paramount importance for promoting positive climate conditions in school settings since they serve to direct program implementation and interpersonal relationships. You need to understand that school board policies specify what it is that your school program is to accomplish. Administrative regulations are the major concern of the professional staff and serve to answer the question of how the policies are to be implemented.

(2) Policy proposals and the drafting of administrative regulations provide an excellent opportunity for you and your staff to participate in the decision-making process of the school and school district. Hold it! Please do not skip this section just yet. We realize that, unfortunately, most school districts nationally purchase their policies and administrative regulations from the National School Boards Association (NSBA).

This boilerplate practice cheats the school district and your school from personalizing the important policies and regulations that govern your practices. It is not the purpose here to detail the many missing opportunities for school districts to develop their own set of policies and regulations, but boilerplate practices tend to curtail important opportunities for school personnel to participate in the school district's decision-making procedures.

(3) Viable school policies are an important communication vehicle for helping you, your staff, and the school's stakeholders understand the school district's aims. Each teacher in your school might have a copy of the school district's policy manual gathering dust on a shelf in their classroom. Next time one of your teachers complains about an important matter dealing with curriculum, student retention, or professional development, ask them if they have read about the matter in the school policy manual. We know what their answer will be. But join them in researching this activity. Our guess is that both of you will learn more about the topic, and it just might lead to other positive actions on your part.

5. Schools with Problem-Solving Capacity Are Associated with Healthy School Climates

Although the creative, healthy organization purposely experiments with new ideas and encourages risk-taking innovation, it invests in basic research, has flexible long-range planning strategies, and implants the feeling of "what would happen if . . . " in the thinking of its employees. Thus, experimentation is purposeful and "controlled" in that a scientific approach is utilized for problem-solving (Norton, 2005, p. 93).

Schools with open and closed climate types both face difficult problems and have personnel conflicts. However, because of the effective system of communication in open school climates, problem and conflict resolution is more likely to be successful. Open channels of communication, the hiring of highly qualified and diversified staff, ad hoc suggestion boxes, pilot programs, task force groups, and brainstorming sessions enable the school leader to be far more able to understand that the school is part of the environment in which it is embedded. Therefore, he or she is continuously in contact with outside sources. In healthy climates, challenges are addressed, solutions to problems are found, and new methods of practice are initiated. Thus, a school with a healthy climate not only implements effective processes but also is more likely to have a high-trust culture.

SUMMARY

Both the research in the field and empirical evidence in practice make it clear that effective school outcomes are much more likely to take place in schools with positive school climates. Furthermore, positive school climates depend largely on the leadership characteristics of the school principal.

Chapter 3 discussed the similarities and differences between school culture and school climate as well as the paramount importance of each phenomenon in influencing the development of important goals and achieving desired educational outcomes. Culture was defined as the set of assumptions, beliefs, values, and attitudes that members of the school or school system share. Culture allows its members to commit themselves to meaningful purposes and superordinate goals above and beyond personal, vested interests. Culture was viewed as being more normative than school climate, and thus culture is not easily changed, if at all. Climate, however, reflects more of the interpersonal relations that take place in the school; it is manifested in the attitude and behaviors of all the members of the school community.

School principals must understand school climate and how it can be assessed because of its influence on such factors as student achievement, job satisfaction, member conflict, staff development, and the morale of students and teachers. In view of its definition, school climate is a phenomenon that can be changed and improved. Climate improvement is inextricably dependent on the positive leadership of the school principal. Several programs and procedures were detailed in the chapter relative to ways in which school climate is improved. School leaders necessarily must give attention to the program, process, and material determinants that characterize the target areas for climate improvement.

A synthesis of the available literature was presented that resulted in several characteristics and/or successful program practices associated with schools with positive climates. A set of shared goals, a viable self-image, high performance expectations, a viable set of school policies and regulations, and opportunities for personal growth and development were found to be present in those schools with open, innovative, and positive school climates.

APPLICATION EXERCISES

1. Walk through every hallway, corridor, office, and conference or meeting room and take inventory of the items, artifacts, papers, pictures, and documents that you see. What message(s) do they seem to convey? What is the basic message that you are receiving? What do the items seem to tell you about your school and your students? Do they suggest any priorities? If so, what are they? Do they reflect positively, negatively, or have no influence on the image and climate of your school? Are they cluttered, hodgepodge, or are they well organized? You might want to include a group of parents in your tour in order to get their views

    Contrast opinions about the messages you want your teachers, students, and visitors to receive. If there is a difference in what the messages are sending and what you desire, develop a plan to involve your students, faculty, and staff in improving the quality and themes of those messages.

    Should some areas of the school contain a particular theme? Should some areas direct the message to particular groups such as teachers, students, parents, or visitors?

2. Develop your own informal school climate checklist relative to what people are saying in regular, routine conversations in your school. Granted, when you walk into the cafeteria or faculty lounge, the conversation might change. Does this tell you anything about the climate in your school? Are comments positive relative to students? Are they encouraging comments about school procedures? Are teachers excited about their classes and student performance? Do students greet you on the campus and/or in the hallways? When at lunch, what do teachers talk to you about or what do they ask you?

    Take time to create a document with two columns; one side with the heading "Positive," and the other side with "Negative." Jot down what you hear over time and think about those areas that need your attention.

3. Conduct an informal assessment of how your front office staff greets, deals with, responds to, or resolves issues with visitors. How does the office staff greet people who appear for help or to ask a question? How long do visitors have to wait to be greeted by staff personnel? How does the office staff handle disgruntled parents? If your school were a for-profit enterprise, would the greeting inspire the customer to return? What are the implications of your observations? Does the office staff deserve a pat on the back? Or is some serious "in-service education" in order?

4. With your school leadership team or randomly selected teachers, bring up the idea of the operational or educational climate of your school. Tell them you want to get a general feeling about the climate at the school and would like to start with the following short survey. Prepare a short handout, perhaps with the questions listed in figure 3.7, and ask them to respond.

    Your analysis of the results of this survey will lead you to the next step. One option is to bring the results of the survey to the leadership team or department or grade level chair meeting. Discuss the results and ask them for direction regarding next steps.

QUESTION	YES	NO
Do teachers in our school feel they are being heard by the administration?		
Are there issues in the school that need to be resolved that have not been addressed?		
If people in our school need help, do they feel they can get it?		
Are front office personnel, including the administrators, perceived to be open, approachable, and helpful?		
Do teachers in our school feel they are supported by the administration?		
Does the overall climate in our school foster, facilitate, or enable teaching and learning?		
Do the teachers in our school really feel a part of the school?		
Do you feel the climate at our school could be improved?		

Figure 3.7. Sample Climate Survey for Teachers

On the other hand, you could administer the Wymore School Climate Assessment instrument set forth in this chapter. In either case, you will have a set of data that you can use to embark on your efforts to create an ideal school climate for learning at your school.

REFERENCES

Alliance for the Study of School Climate (2004). *School Climate Asssessment Instrument (SCAI).* Los Angeles, Calif.: Charter College of Education.

Barnard, C.I. (1938). *The functions of the executive.* Cambridge, Mass.: Harvard University Press.

Barth, R.S. (1990). *Improving schools from within.* San Francisco, Calif.: Jossey-Bass.

Bathhurst, P. (2007, March 11). Training is the key at top firms. *Arizona Republic,* p. ED1.

Clifton, D.O., & Nelson, P. (1992). *Soar with your strengths.* New York: Dell.

Cohen, J. (2007, Fall). Evaluating and improving school climate. *School culture and climate.* Washington, D.C.: National Association of Independent Schools. From http://www.nais.org/publications/ismagazinearticle.cfm?itemNumber=150284.

Covey, S.R. (1996). Three roles of the leader in the new paradigm. In Hesselbein, Goldsmith, & Bechard, R. (Eds.), *The Leader of the Future.* San Francisco, Calif.: Jossey-Bass.

Cuban, L. (1998). How schools change reforms: Redefining reform success and failure. *The Teachers College Record*, 99(3) 453–77.

Deal, T.E., & Peterson, K.D. (1999). *Shaping school culture: The heart of leadership*, San Francisco, Calif.: Jossey-Bass.

Edmonds, R. (1982, December). Programs of school improvement: An overview. *Leadership*, 40, 4–11.

e-Lead (2012, February 27). Creating a learning-centered school climate and culture. In *Leadership for Student Success.* From: http://www.e-lead.org/resources.asp?ResourceID=25.

Halpin, A., & Croft, D.B. (1962). *The organizational climate of schools.* U.S. Office of Education Research Project (Contract #SAE 543-8639). Chicago, Ill.: University of Chicago, Midwest Administration Center.

Hope College (2011, November 2). The Hope College climate survey. *Hope CollegeLGBTNews: Campus Climate, Campus Climate Survey.* Holland, Mich.: Author.

Hopkins, W., & Crain, K. (1985). *The key to an effective school.* Paper presented at the annual meeting of the National Association of Secondary School Principals, New Orleans, La.

Hoy, W.K., & Hannum, J. (1997). Middle school climate: An empirical assessment of organizational health and student achievement. *Educational Administration Quarterly*, 33(3), 290–311.

Jones, P., Yonezawa, S., Mehan, H., & McClure, L. (2008). *School climate and student achievement.* California Department of Education. Davis, Calif.: University of California at Davis.

Koenig, B. (2012, February 27). Culture and climate at school. *Psychology Articles.* From: http://www.freepsychologyarticles.com/culture-and-climate-at-school.html.

Kotter, J.P., & Heskett, J.L. (1992). *Corporate culture and performance.* New York: The Free Press, A Division of the Macmillan Company.

Leithwood, K.A., & Montgomery, D.J. (1984, April). *Patterns of growth in principal effectiveness.* Paper presented at the annual meeting of AERA, New Orleans, La.

Lezotte, K.A., & McKee-Snyder (2004). *Implementation guide: Assembly required: A continuous school improvement system.* Okemos, Mich.: Effective Schools Products, Ltd.

Lezotte, L.W., & McKee-Snyder, K. (2011). *What effective schools do: Re-envisioning the correlates.* Bloomington, Ind.: Solutions Tree.

Lunenburg, F.C., & Ornstein, A.C. (2004). *Educational administration: Concepts and practices* (4th ed.). Belmont, Calif.: Wadsworth/Thompson.

McGregor, D. (1960). *The human side of enterprise.* New York: McGraw-Hill.

Morgan, G. (1986). *Images of organization.* Newbury Park, Calif.: Sage.

National Association of Secondary School Principals (1987). *CASE survey.* Reston, Va.: Author.

National School Climate Center (2012). *School Climate.* New York: National School Climate Center.

Norton, M.S. (2005). *Executive leadership for effective administration.* Boston, Mass.: Allyn & Bacon.

Norton, M.S. (2008). *Human resources for educational leaders.* Thousand Oaks, Calif.: Sage.

Ornstein, A.C., & Levine, D.U. (2003). *Foundations of education* (8th ed.). Boston, Mass.: Houghton Mifflin.

Owens, R.G. (2004). *Organizational behavior in education: Adaptive leadership and school reform* (8th ed.). Boston, Mass.: Allyn & Bacon.

Paredes, V., & Frazier, L. (1992). *School climate in AISD.* Independent School District, Austin, Tex.: Office of Research and Evaluation.

Phi Delta Kappa (1973). *School climate improvement: A challenge to the school administrator.* Bloomington, Ind.: Author.

Plamondon, W.N. (1996). Energy and Leadership. In Hesselbein, Goldsmith, & Bechard (Eds.), *The Leader of the Future.* San Francisco, Calif.: Jossey-Bass, p. 277.

Purkey, S.C., & Smith, M.S. (1983). Effective schools: A review. *The Elementary School Journal,* 83(4), 427–52.

Robinson, W., & Buntrock, L.M. (2011). Leading a school turnaround. *The School Administrator,* 681(3), 22–27.

Rutherford, W.J. (1985). School principals as effective leaders. *Phi Delta Kappa,* 67, 31–34.

Shindler, J., Jones, A., Williams, D., Taylor, C., & Cadenas, H. (2009). *Exploring the school climate-student achievement connection: And making sense of why the first precedes the second.* Alliance for the Study of School Climate. Los Angeles, Calif.: California State University.

Stedman, L. (1987). It's time we change the effective schools formula. *Educational Leadership,* 69(3), 215–24.

Stern, G.G. (1964). *High school characteristics index.* Syracuse, N.Y.: Psychological Research Center, Syracuse University.

Sweeney, J. (1992). The key to excellence. *NASSP Bulletin,* 76, 69–73.

Tead, O., & Metcalf, H.C. (1920). *Personnel administration.* New York: McGraw-Hill.

Wynne, E.A. (1981). Looking at good schools. *Phi Delta Kappan,* 62, 377–81.

4

ROLES AND RESPONSIBILITIES FOR ESTABLISHING A POSITIVE LEARNING ENVIRONMENT

It is almost impossible to read an article on education today without seeing the terms *school learning climate* or *school-community learning culture*. We discussed this topic in relation to the importance of the school's climate and culture in the previous chapter. Our purpose in this chapter is to extend this concept in relation to the additional challenges that you face in establishing a learning climate and culture in your school and the community.

We begin by discussing the topic of the teacher as a learning-leader and the contributions that he or she can make to improvements in student achievement. The vital importance of parental support of student learning at home and how it can be accomplished is emphasized. We discuss the responsibilities of students for their own learning.

A school-community learning culture requires accountability on the part of many groups and individuals. How must you, the principal, be held accountable for student achievement in the school? How should teachers be held accountable as well as parents, partners, and other stakeholders in the community?

The final section of the chapter centers on building effective school and community partnerships. How would you assess your school's partnership relations with various individuals and groups in the community? Are such partnerships in existence? Why are they effective or not so effective? Of what relevance is the establishment of collaboratives for student achievement? We address these questions in this chapter.

CHAPTER 4

LEARNING ENVIRONMENT: TEACHERS AS LEARNING-LEADERS

We asked selected principals the question, "How do you gain the commitment of faculty and staff toward the establishment of a learning culture in the school?" A common response by principal learning-leaders centered on the concept of honesty. It was okay for them to admit that they didn't know the answer to a question posed. You can build trust by being honest about your lack of personal knowledge regarding a question relative to student learning and then working next to the individual or group in an attempt to learn the answer.

Honesty should go farther as well. When you complete a class walkthrough, for example, you need to be honest about what you see. You might have to tell the teacher, "I saw this. What we need to see is this instead. I want to see it working in your classroom immediately. Here's how I am going to help you."

Before sharing several of the principals' responses concerning promoting a learning environment in the classroom, take a few minutes now to think about your behavior in this regard. How do or would you promote a learning culture in the classroom? Here are several learning-leaders' responses to this faculty commitment question:

P-1. The principal must be willing to do what he or she asks others to do. Be honest about your own knowledge and learn yourself. I am an active participant in the professionals' and the school's learning activities. The staff sees me involved and taking notes. Such involvement results in trust. I work with the staff to demonstrate what I have just learned.

I hold high expectations for the students, the staff, and myself. We were using the term *excellence* somewhat casually. I asked the staff, "Do we really believe in excellence as our goal?" Then I asked them, "What does excellence mean to you? I gave them one full week to write their personal definitions of excellence. I wanted each teacher (T) to give thought to his or her definition. The following responses are a few of those submitted to me.

T-1. Excellence is challenging each student to reach the highest level that he or she is capable of achieving. The teacher helps students meet the challenge by providing instruction at an appropriate level for them. It is a team of teachers who work collaboratively to support each other and all the students at that grade or subject level.

T-2. Excellence is pushing yourself to perform at a level that you didn't even think you could achieve (in all aspects of life). Excellence is never thinking that you are doing good enough. You can always get better.

T-3. Excellence is making whatever difference you can make with the gifts and talents you've been given. It is working as a team to support the gifts and talents of others. It is being true to who you are with every thought, word, and action.

T-4. Excellence to me is a teacher who not only is successful at getting students to grow academically but one that makes life fuller and more satisfying for each learner.

T-5. Excellence is a conscious decision to act with integrity at all times. It is giving our best to whatever we do. When we practice excellence, we experience joy and peace.

T-6. True excellence is that state when one reaches maximum self-fulfillment. Excellence is a motivator in the sense that we might never fully reach it as a goal, but we do realize personal satisfaction and success in our continuous progress toward that goal. As excellence relates to our students, we set high expectations for their achievement in hope that each individual student will be motivated to do their very best in relation to their given talents and personal interests.

T-7. Excellence is realized when an individual or group meets and/or exceeds predetermined goals and objectives. When a school staff sets and agrees on a goal based on high academic expectations and reaches or exceeds that goal, we can say that it did an excellent job.

The definitions themselves were important only because the activity made each of us give serious thought to who we are, why we exist, and what we want to achieve. The term *excellence* comes up in most every faculty improvement meeting scheduled. We were able to make a commitment to the goal of reaching excellence in helping each student become a successful learner.

P-2. One of the most important ways to foster a learning culture in the school is to be a learner yourself. I take every opportunity possible to learn and then bring that information back to the staff. I always loved teaching and so I often demonstrate a skill or concept that I have learned by using it in a classroom. I like serving as an instructional coach. These behaviors, I think, give me more credibility with my teaching staff. I often sit with achievement teams in order to learn from them.

P-3. I always try to be honest about my own knowledge. I am not afraid to learn myself. Teachers see me involved in various in-service activities, taking notes and reporting back to them. I am willing to do whatever I ask my teachers to do. I believe there is a trust factor that results in their knowing that I know that I don't know it all. I am quick to praise the good work that I see someone doing and do my best to keep criticism at a minimum.

P-4. The staff knows that I believe every grade level owns every other grade level. Our learning improvement meetings are good data meetings when all teachers look at the achievement of all children. Student achievement in every grade is an open book. We discuss openly the pluses and minuses of student progress. In the many cases when student achievement is not progressing as expected, teachers ask questions about what the class is doing, what methods are being used, and then take the time to provide suggestions.

I often suggest that the teacher in question observe another teacher. I watch closely for timely occasions when I can recommend that other teachers take the opportunity to visit him or her as well.

P-5. I believe that the key word is *expectations*. I do my best to foster high expectations in the thinking of teachers, parents, and the school community. I open the gate for each staff member to move ahead with agreed-upon achievement objectives. I make sure that they have resources to implement their teaching methods. I make every effort to find the right staff personnel and make it clear to them what it will take to remain at our school.

We have a school-community approach. On registration day, we commonly have parents camping outside the school overnight to get a seat for their child in the school. We explain to each parent who we are and what we expect of each child. For example, we have a contract agreement with the parents of each student. Parents must give the school twenty hours of service in order to keep their kids in our school. We ask them, "What can you do for our school, our teachers, or our school community?" In some cases, we have to tell them that our school might not be right for their child.

How You Can Foster Teacher Learning-Leadership in Your School

The topic of the teacher as a learning-leader can be considered from at least two perspectives. One perspective is that of the teacher being an outstanding teacher: one who is student centered in his or her classroom instruction. That is, the teacher utilizes the student's personal interests and needs to guide decisions relative to what is taught and what instructional methods are used. The teacher is able to see things from the student's viewpoint, stands up for student rights, creates a classroom environment in which students can focus on their interests and strengths, and uses a nonpunitive approach in student disciplinary matters (Norton, Kelly, & Battle, 2012).

Another perspective of the teacher learning-leader is the individual who is a learning-leader beyond the four walls of the classroom. This teacher might be interested in pursuing a future career in school administration or one who remains in the classroom. The latter assumes learning-leadership through special contributions as a resource teacher, designing curriculum, giving instructional demonstrations, chairing a school improvement team, putting a new intervention into practice, serving as a coach or mentor for other teachers in the school or school district, or just helping other teachers achieve a personal learning goal.

Figure 4.1 reveals some of the ways that your teacher leaders can serve both teachers and students. A teacher leader might be active in one or more of the activity areas.

As school principal, you have an important role in identifying, encouraging, and supporting quality teacher learning-leaders. Teachers indeed are human and might feel uneasy about working closely with you as school administrator. Some believe that it is not "cool" to be collaborating with administrators, especially in their own school. You must be careful that teacher learning-leaders are not uncomfortable in the role or looked upon by other staff as being favored. You should tap the potential teacher leader on the shoulder and encourage their service in the same way that you select a teacher as a class sponsor or for heading up a special learning session for school parents.

"Teachers who feel they are respected as educational leaders are more effective in and out of the classroom" (Century Learning, 2002, p. 5). In fact, teacher leaders can be a positive force toward reaching achievement goals and the implementation of a learn-

Areas of Learning Activities

Designing Curriculum

Coaching & Mentoring

Serving as a Resource Teacher

Helping Teachers Reach Goals

Chairing an Improvement Team

Demonstrating Teaching Methods

Testing a Recommended Intervention

Observing Other Teachers on the Teacher's Request

Explaining School's Achievement Data Results to Stakeholders

Serving as Data Analyzer for Grade Levels or Subject Matter Areas

Figure 4.1. Selected Areas of Teacher Leader Activities

ing culture in the school. After all, who is better prepared to mentor potential teacher leaders than you?

Just having a mission statement that says your school believes in learning for all students or just saying to the staff that they should collaborate is not sufficient. You need to develop a model for assessing student achievement, determining the gaps between the present status of student achievement and desired achievement goals, and then taking action that implements a plan to reduce the achievement gap that most likely exists. We present guidelines for implementing such a plan later in this chapter.

In one case, a learning-leader principal stated that over time, twenty-five of the school's sixty teachers could be considered teacher learning-leaders. Such an accomplishment necessitates a healthy climate and sustained efforts. Such efforts include such activities as providing opportunities for teachers to learn from one another. In some instances, a stand is taken against the use of excuses for not implementing student-centered learning in the classroom.

It is important for the principal to help teachers become comfortable with using data to assess instructional effectiveness. One-on-one mentoring sessions between the teacher and principal during the teacher's prep period can serve as an opportune time for data analysis instruction. Once the teacher becomes comfortable with data analysis, he or she can use achievement results for their own self-evaluation and performance improvement.

Learning Snapshot #1—The Lincoln School District was establishing a representative team of middle school teachers to examine the current math program and make

CHAPTER 4

recommendations for improvement. The Southeast Middle School math staff consisted of six teachers. Carl Maddox was one of them.

Principal Virginia O'Brian was asked to appoint one of the Southeast math teachers as a member of the district team. She thought about Carl as a possible team member. He was the only math teacher that was not serving on any other school-related team or busy with another school activity. She thought that the experience might be good for him.

When she approached Carl about serving on the district team, Carl was against it. "Those so-called district improvement teams are a waste of time. I served on one of them a few years ago and could hardly wait to get it over," said Carl. "Let someone else do it."

Principal O'Brian responded that other math teachers were quite involved in other projects and that he was the logical one to serve this time. Carl attended the first district meeting reluctantly. He sat back slumped in his chair, obviously upset that he had to be there. His behavior during the next two meetings was similar; apathy was evident.

At one point during the fourth meeting of the math team, the team was discussing the specific content of a course in beginning algebra. That conversation sparked a first verbal comment from Carl. "I use a method of teaching that has worked quite well for me," he asserted. He briefly explained the method to the other team members. He saw the heads of other team members shaking in approval of the method. Miss Farman, the district office curriculum coordinator, remarked: "I like that idea a great deal. We could put it in our enrichment section of the curriculum guide. Carl, would you be willing to write that up for us?"

For the first time, Carl sat up straight in his seat with a smile on his face. His new attitude at future meetings was evident. He became a valuable contributor to the curriculum team. When it came time to organize a subcommittee on math resources to be selected, who was the first member to volunteer?

When the work of the math committee was completed, Carl became a leading resource for the other five math teachers at Southeast. In this capacity he served as a valuable teacher leader.

Who benefited from this experience? Virtually everyone. Carl certainly benefited, the math team benefited, the school district and Southeast Middle School benefited, and the other math teachers in Carl's school benefited as well. What about the students? We have to assume that Carl's reengagement in the school district's learning culture benefited his students and other students in the school district as well.

ACCOUNTABILITY: PROVIDING ACHIEVEMENT EVIDENCE THAT COUNTS AND WHAT LEARNING ACCOUNTABILITY MEANS

By 2001, most every state had established some system of accountability for student achievement. Some states use public reporting systems. Others use locally defined accountability systems or accountability systems defined by the state. Achievement progress is viewed differently among the states. For example, in some states progress is defined in relation to meeting an absolute target of achievement performance. Some states account for achievement progress by setting an annual growth target based on last year's achievement performance. In any case, the accountability requirements for student learning often appear to be overwhelming.

Another view of progress is that of examining the achievement gap. That is, has the school reduced the number or percentage of students with the lowest scores compared to last year's tests (Goertz & Duffy, 2001)?

State assessment tests serve as the primary measures of student achievement. Student proficiency assessments in mathematics and English language arts or reading are most common through the majority of states. Achievement assessments also are practiced in science, written composition, and social studies by the majority of states. In fewer instances, noncognitive measures are implemented for student attendance, dropout rates, and student retention in grade.

What is your definition of the term *accountability*? Take a minute to write it down. Does your definition of the term reflect Webster's definition: "an obligation or willingness to accept responsibility or to account for one's actions"? We would not argue with the dictionary definition, and the following are examples of how several principal learning-leaders defined the term *accountability*. Check your definition against the ones that we collected.

P-1. In regard to student achievement, great success is related to teacher accountability. Poor success is related to the principal's lack of accountability. He or she did not give good support to teachers or students.

P-2. Accountability is a positive concept for true learning-leaders. They want to be responsible for their primary job role: that of showing evidence of continuous student academic progress. Some principals that I know say it's a dirty word. I disagree.

P-3. In a learning school culture, grade team members hold one another accountable for student achievement results. This means that when the team misses the mark, it looks at itself rather than blaming others. However, accountability requires the team to not only examine achievement results, but to analyze those procedures that were successful and those procedures that were not.

P-4. Accountability is being practiced when the individual is involved in the determination of the learning achievement goals for the class and/or individuals, plays a significant role in implementing instructional procedures, and has a part in the use of several means of assessing student progress. The individual is then held responsible for providing evidence that learning goals were met or exceeded. Lack of progress necessitates a cyclical return to determining new learning achievement goals and making new efforts to achieve them.

P-5. Accountability is a hot potato. If the learning program for an individual or group of students results in reaching achievement benchmarks, then it's considered to be a sweet potato and everyone wants to handle it hot or not.

CHAPTER 4

If the achievement benchmarks are not realized, well, no one wants to handle a hot potato. Nevertheless, accountability is upon us. It is our responsibility to know when our methods are truly serving to meet our main objective of improved student learning.

TEACHER ABSENTEEISM AND PROFESSIONAL ACCOUNTABILITY

Each of these learning-leader "definitions" is interesting, but for our purposes, as previously noted, we accept Webster's definition of accountability: the acceptance of responsibility for one's own actions. Does this definition cover teacher behavior that has the potential to affect student achievement? We believe that it does. Think, for example, about the matter of teacher absenteeism. What difference does it make whether teachers are in the classroom with the learners or not? Is it being accountable on the part of a teacher when he or she takes advantage of accrued sick leave before losing it?

Several studies over the years have reported that teacher absenteeism impacts negatively on student achievement (Miller, Murnane, & Willett, 2007; Pitkoff, 1993; Summers & Raivaetz, 1982). Each study by these authorities revealed that teacher absences have a significant educational impact on student achievement.

Unless the school district's leave policy provides for unlimited accrual of sick leave time and such time is reimbursed upon retirement, empirical evidence suggests that the sick leave policy is often abused. In one study by Norton (Webb & Norton, 2004), human resources directors named teacher absenteeism of staff among the leading ten major problems facing them. If sick leave and other absence policies are abused and teachers are out of the classroom, it is likely that it lessens student-learning opportunities. Our message here is simple and straightforward: commitment to student learning involves many factors. Absenteeism is one of those factors, and therefore it must be monitored.

Later in the chapter, we will discuss more specifically the process of demonstrating accountability for student achievement. In the following section, the focus is that of monitoring student achievement and analyzing achievement results.

WHY YOU NEED TO GIVE ATTENTION TO STUDENT LEARNING STYLES

A common expectation set forth by various federal and state agencies is that every student can and should gain one year of learning in one year of schooling. We support the goal as a learning standard; it does appear to be logical. It's just that we agree with other authorities that learning does not always occur in a "building block," linear manner. Cognitive psychology suggests that learning occurs in various ways. For some students it is more like "Tinkertoys" or networking. What about your own learning style? Do you usually try to visualize the task before moving ahead on it? Do you learn better in a linear, step-by-step fashion? That is, would you have had to learn addition before you tackled subtraction? Or could you have learned the four arithmetical processes in any order?

Several styles of learning do not follow the basic sequential style that is most practiced in our classrooms. Our traditional grade level organization is structured much in the same way: first grade, second grade, third grade, and so forth. We're really not comfortable with any other arrangement. Abstract learners, on the other hand, learn in no particular order. It is beyond the scope of this chapter to discuss in detail the full gamut of learning style theory. But let's illustrate the importance of this consideration by examining the learning differences between *concrete sequential* learners and *abstract sequential* learners as set forth by Anthony Gregorc (2011).

The student that is primarily a concrete sequential learner likes order, logical sequence, following directions, and getting information and facts built sequentially. This is exemplified by the common procedures of learning addition, then subtraction, then multiplication, and finally division. The common belief is that the student must know multiplication before they tackle division. The fact is that division is as closely tied to subtraction as it is to multiplication (e.g., 10 divided by 2 = 5; 10 - 2 = 8; 8 - 2 = 6; 6 - 2 = 4; 4 - 2 = 2; and 2 - 2 = 0. We subtracted 2 from 10 exactly 5 times).

As Gregorc (2011) points out, concrete sequential learners learn best when it is structured. Learning is facilitated for them when they can work with others to do an assignment and when the learning situation is predictable. Having too many options is problematic for them. They need specific directions for completing the assignment. They have difficulty working with abstract ideas or assignments that demand using one's imagination. Frustration can occur when questions posed have no right or wrong answers.

Now let's compare learning situations for an abstract sequential learner who likes to analyze situations before making a decision. This learner likes applying logic in problem-solving situations. They most often work best on their own but like to have access to expert information in reference material. They prefer to work in stimulating environments that challenge them to find solutions to problems. Frustration for them can occur when they have to repeat the same lessons over and over, do not have time to consider the subject thoroughly, or are working with others who do not accept their point of view.

David Kolb (2011) provides us with another perspective of human learning that tends to support Gregorc's work. Kolb points out that it is natural for different people to prefer one particular learning style. Although we oversimplify Kolb's learning-styles model, it includes four distinct learning preferences: *diverging* or feeling and watching; *assimilating* or watching and thinking; *converging* or doing and thinking; and *accommodating* or doing and feeling. For example, students with a diverging style prefer to watch rather than do. Students with an accommodating style prefer a "hands-on" learning experience. They set targets and try different ways to solve a problem.

CHAPTER 4

The foregoing discussion is only a small part of the complex considerations regarding learning theory. The crux of the matter is that students as individuals learn differently; one teacher's instructional style might be much better for some students than others. In fact, the teacher's style might be inhibiting the learning progress for some students.

We submit that a major feature of individualization is that of working to find the learning style of each student and then doing whatever is necessary to teach him or her using the style that is in tune with the learner. True learning-leaders understand this and do whatever is necessary to implement various classroom assessments in an attempt to find out how a student learns best. This is part of what we mean by being student-centered and making learning decisions to meet the needs and best interests of each student. When you find the best learning style for the student and use it in the classroom, student achievement improves. This is what we mean when we talk about a positive learning climate.

Learning Snapshot #2—One of Alex's favorite subjects is American history. He asks good questions in class and contributes to the class discussions. However, his semester grade in the course was a C primarily due to low test scores. For example, he commonly receives scores of B on multiple choice- and matching date-type questions but receives a D or F on essay-type questions. Mr. Stortz, his teacher, brought this to the attention of the school's social studies teaching team. One member of the team commented, "That's the way it goes. Some students just can't write. I don't know what they are doing in elementary school nowadays to teach these kids how to express themselves in writing."

However, Miss Hurst asked if Alex might be given the essay portion of the tests orally. Mr. Stortz instituted this idea immediately. Alex's grade jumped to B on essay portions of the tests thereafter.

Empirical and research evidence also supports the contention that some students have difficulty processing instruction that is given orally. Since so much of your teachers' instruction is given orally, this might be a learning problem for some students in your school.

ACCOUNTABILITY AND PRESENTING EVIDENCE THAT REALLY COUNTS

As you are aware, school districts, individual schools, principals, and teachers are being held accountable for what and how students learn in school today. Due to its importance, we have touched on the topic of accountability in each chapter of this book. In the following section, emphasis is given to accountability in terms of how it is being addressed in practice and what principal learning-leaders do to provide learning evidence that really counts.

ESTABLISHING A POSITIVE LEARNING ENVIRONMENT

Assume that you are attending a meeting on student achievement. Other school principals, central office curriculum supervisors, representative parents, and three school board representatives also are present. One parent representative asks, "Just how are our teachers being held accountable for their students' learning results?" Then a school board member says, "Yes, and just what are school principals doing relative to their learning accountability responsibilities?"

The school superintendent responds, "Any of our school principals can answer those questions. Principal Jones, please take the lead and give us your answers to those two questions." Okay, let's take a break. Take some time now to note your likely response to the two questions posed. Draft a quick outline that lists the key points of your response.

The following briefs are responses to the parent's question above: "Just how are our teachers being held accountable for their student learning results?" Of course, the following practice examples are partial responses and do not give a complete picture of all the things that are done to gather data, analyze the data, and make appropriate changes to improve student learning.

Principal Response #1. I keep a student-learning chart for each classroom teacher's students and their learning progress for English, reading, math, and science. For example, the chart gives the number of students in each classroom and the number of students above the standard learning score benchmark (AB), those at the benchmark (B), and those below the benchmark (BM) for each of the four subject areas. Thus for the sixth-grade teacher who has twenty-six children in the class, my chart might show data for reading such as 10 AB, 9 B, and 7 BM.

The student's classroom achievement record is monitored frequently to determine his or her changing achievement status. Collected classroom data and other standard tests are used to determine learning progress and/or the need for some intervention.

Learning improvement sessions are held on an ongoing basis. Those students below benchmark standards (BM) are given special attention and adjustments made in their learning program and methods. Just because a student scores above the benchmark (AB) does not mean that they do not get full attention. Rather, it is the staff's philosophy to have all students progressing according to their potential.

Principal Response #2. We schedule common planning time (CPT) for grade level teams to meet at least once every two weeks. In each instance, the improvement team considers all the students in each of the grades represented. That is, a teacher is not only concerned about his or her own students (see figure 4.2). Every grade level owns every grade level. All teachers look at all children.

I have a copy of the CPT Summary that each team completes and submits to me following each meeting. I ask for specifics relative to such topics as successful teaching methods that were used. Such information is then shared among the team members. Assessments that were made to collect specific achievement data are reported, and interventions relative to program arrangements and special student grouping are reported.

CHAPTER 4

Date of Meeting:

Time (Start and Finish):

Team Members in Attendance:

Topic(s) of Discussion:

Data (Student Grouping/Regrouping):

Differentiation:

Assessments:

Interventions (Grouping/Regrouping):

Follow-Up Considerations:

Decisions and/or Conclusions Reached:

Next CPT Time:

Focus:

Materials Needed:

Special Communication Needed (Principal, Parents, Others):

Special Follow-Up Responsibilities:

Figure 4.2. Common Planning Team (CPT) Summary
Source: Adapted from the CPT Summary Form used by the Fuller Elementary School, Tempe Elementary School District, Ken White, principal. Tempe, Arizona. Used with permission.

Before each team meeting adjourns, the team determines the focus of the next meeting and makes team member assignments as fits the case. Materials that are needed for instructional purposes and the persons responsible for follow-up on various matters are appointed. These summary team reports serve several purposes. Of course, they serve to keep all of us focused on our primary task of student learning. They suggest both successful practices that we have in place and those that are not proving to be effective.

The team meetings have given new energy to the collaborative efforts of our teachers and provide opportunities for each team member to learn of successful practices being used by their co-workers. New interventions are commonly demonstrated first by one or more teachers in the classroom. All of this looms important in establishing the school's learning culture.

Principal Response #3. Every teacher in our school uses a data notebook. He or she uses the notebook to help determine daily lessons, the success of instructional methods used, and progress toward individual student benchmarks. Every teacher keeps a "pocket chart" to keep achievement data current and easily available. If any student is not making satisfactory progress, this is revealed almost immediately. The teacher and the members of his or her teaching team examine the student's achievement data and set forth a plan in writing. In most every instance, the student's parents are contacted when changes are determined so that they can be prepared to support the intervention at their level.

So we have our data in front at all times. We keep records of the interventions used and keep our eye on what has worked and what has not worked. Although we encourage controlled risk taking, we are quick to change gears when it is apparent that the new intervention is not producing achievement results. Using a variety of achievement assessment strategies serves to avoid the misuse of data by using only one indicator.

Yes, sometimes I worry about our drowning in assessments. At some point it seems best to just "shut off the lights and go to bed." Don't misunderstand, but you must determine what data generated by the teacher really is most accurate and useful and then use it to supplement data required by the school board and state and federal agencies.

I want to point out that we teach courses other than the core courses. We teach many things that are not tested such as art, music, civics, and health. In our learning culture, we hold ourselves accountable for teaching the whole child.

Principal Response #4. In reality, we're held accountable for how well students learn in school by most every individual, group, and agency that has any interest at all in education. The feds, I should say the federal government agencies, state government agencies, school board, parents groups, businesses, and other individuals all hold us accountable for student achievement. But I am serious when I say that my staff and I hold ourselves accountable for student learning.

Let me give you an example of a speech that I gave to a local business club last semester. After a few introductory comments regarding student achievement at our local high school and our goal to ensure achievement progress for all students, I showed slides of our students' achievement progress using data from our local classrooms, the state AIMS Test, and the federal school grade-rating for our high school. I used the school's achievement progress chart as evidence that achievement in our basic subjects of math, English, and science had increased from the last evaluation in 2010.

Since the audience consisted mainly of businesspeople, I used their business term, *return on investment (ROI)*, to demonstrate how the cost of initiating one intervention in the English composition class had increased student achievement by nearly 22 percent. The intervention was that of inviting persons from the various occupations such as the state newspapers, publications companies, and book authors to teach one to five classes in writing appropriate to their fields. A small honorarium and travel and lodging expenses were paid to each consultant.

CHAPTER 4

CHARTING STUDENTS' READING PROGRESS THROUGH THE GRADES

Many excellent testing service companies are available for assessing student achievement progress. In some states specific tests are mandated annually. Mandated tests commonly are supplemented by other assessments provided by for-profit and not-for-profit organizations such as the Northwest Evaluation Association (NWEA).

The Norris School District in Nebraska does an outstanding job of informing parents about the school's student achievement assessment procedures. In their communication to parents set forth in their flyer, *A Parent's Guide to the NWEA Assessments*, the school district gives the following information to parents and other stakeholders (Norris School District, 2011).

NWEA works with educational organizations worldwide to provide research-based, computerized adaptive assessments for reading, language usage, and mathematics.

When taking a MAP (Measures of Academic Progress) assessment, the difficulty of each question is based on how well the student answers the previous questions. When questions are answered correctly, the questions get more difficult. When answered incorrectly, questions get easier. The final score is an estimate of the student's achievement level.

NWEA assessments provide a percentile score that compares a student's performance to that of the norm group. It also results in a percentile rank that shows how well the student performed in comparison to students in the norm group. For example, a student with a percentile rank of 62 scored as well or better than 62 percent of the students in the norm group. Such data are of great help in analyzing the status of each student and making decisions regarding his or her learning targets for future learning.

Tests developed by NWEA use a scale to measure student achievement growth termed Rasch UnIT (RIT). The score is directly related to the curriculum scale in each subject area. RIT scores are especially helpful to the school staff, since they can be added together to determine class and school achievement averages. RIT scores range from 100 to 280. Scores of 180 to 200 typically start in grade 3.

A school staff would determine a target score for a student's progress in grade 3 depending on the RIT score of the individual student. All students would be expected to demonstrate progress in achievement. By high school the RIT score typically would range from 220 to 260. Although individual schools and/or school districts commonly set the standards required for student achievement, individual states also set achievement standards for schools.

The foregoing information is not presented to endorse NWEA or any other assessment association. Rather, our primary purpose is to underscore the importance of informing ourselves, parents, and other community stakeholders as to how the school is monitoring their students' achievement progress.

In the Norris parent guide, several tips are set forth for parents as well. Its purpose is to give parents ways to help their child optimize their learning experience. For example, one tip suggests the following: discuss your child's progress with his or her teacher. Ask the teacher to suggest activities for you and your child to do at home to help improve your child's performance. When parents and teachers work together purposely, students are the benefactors.

YOUR STUDENTS MUST HAVE A ROLE IN THEIR OWN LEARNING: GIVING THEM RESPONSIBILITY

Learning-centered schools must hold high expectations for students, but not just for academic performance. Social and moral behavior requires high expectations as well. One middle school in Arizona implements this concept through their program PRIDE: Preparation, Respect, Integrity, Dedication, and Excellence. The program is based on the ideal of heightening the student's ability and refining that ability to achieve excellence.

A rather simple strategy for helping your students assume responsibility is through such activities as keeping their own *tracking charts*. For example, let's use the skill of reading fluency to demonstrate this strategy. The teacher prepares reading passages that are used by pairs of students. One student reads the passage, and his or her partner serves as the timer. Each student keeps a personal progress chart. The date of each reading and the words read per minute are recorded on a line chart. Fluency progress over time can be seen immediately on the chart. Students tend to be motivated to keep their line chart moving upward (see figure 4.3).

Figure 4.4 is an adaptation of one of the components of the PRIDE model to fit any middle school.

Mednick (2003) gives us a great opportunity to stop and think about a student's ownership of his or her own learning. As she notes, "It is a simple but profound concept: to teach our students most effectively we must know them" (p. 4). Mednick suggests that we get to know students by sharing our concerns, passions, and stories with them; by listening to their interests, stories, needs, and dreams; by asking them what they like to do and what's on their minds; by observing how they work and associate with others; and by allowing students' interests and concerns to be part of the curriculum.

But hold on a minute. Can we trust young adolescents to participate in school issues other than planning a school dance or presenting a school assembly program? Mednick (2003) thinks so, and so do Atkinson and Sturges (2003), who believe that young adolescents can indeed have a role in discussing such important issues as teaching and learning, adult and student relationships, and differences in the backgrounds of students attending the school. How might you find out? You ask them!

You will think of other strategies to increase a student's responsibility for his or her own learning. Another example in practice is having the student walk their parents

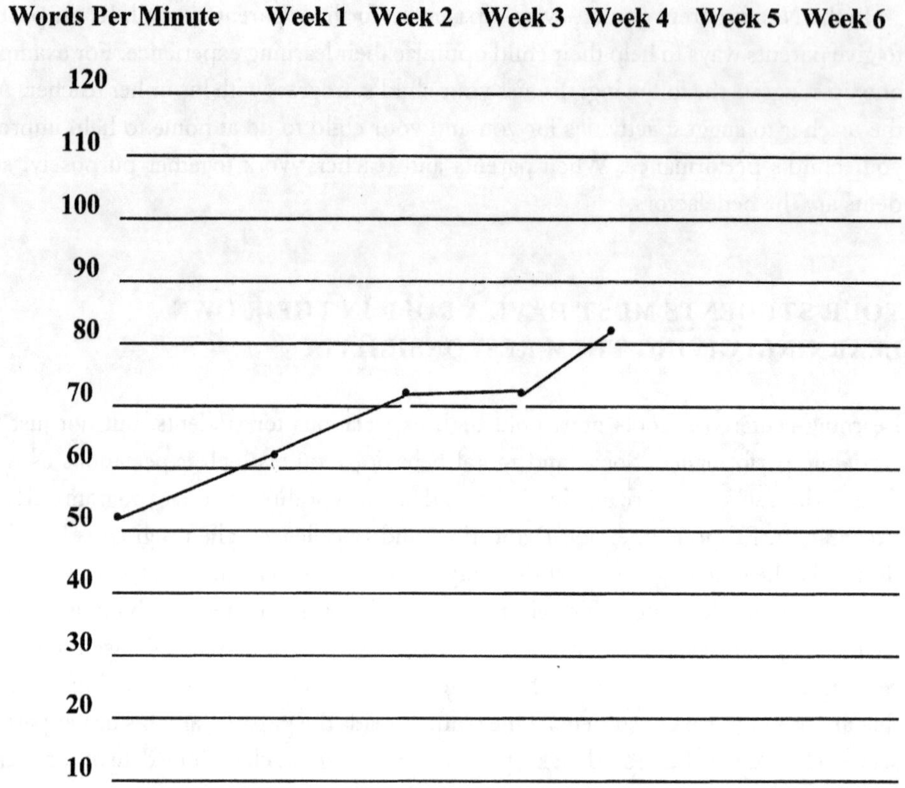

CHAPTER 4

| Words Per Minute | Week 1 | Week 2 | Week 3 | Week 4 | Week 5 | Week 6 |

```
120 _____
110 _____
100 _____
 90 _____
 80 _____
 70 _____
 60 _____
 50 _____
 40 _____
 30 _____
 20 _____
 10 _____
```

Starting Level on 9-5   WPM 50

Goal for 6 weeks time period: 95 WPM

Name:_____   **Partner:**_____

Figure 4.3. Progress Chart for Student Reading

through their portfolio at parent-teacher conferences or on other occasions. The student goes through the portfolio and shows work on which he or she did very well and other information that demonstrates learning progress.

What about homework assignments when a student is absent? One learning-leader explained that the student was held responsible for finding out about homework that was missed. The rationale? The student owns their own learning; they must assume the responsibility for it. Of course, such strategies depend in large part on the age of the student. Such a practice makes more sense when the student is in grade 4 or above.

Students in the Classroom

Preparation
- Be emotionally and mentally ready to learn.
- Bring class materials and completed homework.
- Be on time in your seat ready to learn.
- Keep yourself organized and focused on learning.
- Read and follow any and all instructions on the board.
- Get any absentee work.
- Take note of homework assignment given verbally or on the board.

Respect
- Follow directions the first time.
- Be on task.
- Give your attention to others who are asking questions or contributing to the lesson.
- Treat others with respect. Use kind words.
- Participate appropriately in class discussions or in group activities.

Integrity
- Be honest and make good choices.
- Be responsible for doing your best.
- Be a role model for others.
- Help others in the class when circumstances call for it.

Dedication
- Be an active listener.
- Learn something new every day.
- Ask yourself if you did give it your best.

Excellence
- Do your personal best.
- Encourage others to do their best.
- Turn in all class work complete, neat, and on time.
- Keep a record of your achievement progress on quizzes, tests, homework, and other assignments.
- Have a positive attitude.

Figure 4.4. Students and Their Responsibility for Their Own Learning: PRIDE
Source: Adapted from the 2011–2012 Ward Traditional Academy Handbook. Ward Traditional Academy, Tempe, Arizona. Adapted by permission. (Note: In the Classroom is only one component of the PRIDE model. Other components include In the Hallways, In the Library, On the School Grounds, At an Assembly, In the Cafeteria, and others.)

Not all practices work in every school. Situations differ, and thus your practices might differ. In any case, helping each student learn about responsibility is best implemented in your school while the student is in his or her early years. Parents shouldn't be doing everything for the student when it would be much better in the long run for the student if they would help the student become more responsible. Tell your students, "You are the learners; learning is about you." Celebrate when students take responsibility and do their own work. Foster student independence. Students must put forth the effort to learn!

CHAPTER 4

SUMMARY OF THE SCHOOL'S ACCOUNTABILITY SYSTEMS

A beneficial procedure for assessing a school's accountability system was set forth by Guth and others in 1999 (see figure 4.5). The framework serves a good purpose in summarizing this chapter. The basis of the framework is founded on the content standards of the school's program offerings and instructional methods. Performance standards represent student achievement expectations. Professional development activities for staff personnel must be aligned with the content standards. School principals also must be certain that the school's content standards are aligned with standards set by the state and/or other governing bodies.

Assessments that are aligned with content standards are essential for determining if content standards are actually being taught. These ongoing reviews of student learning serve several purposes. A variety of tests and assessments is utilized to determine areas of positive student achievement results and also those program areas where appropriate interventions are needed to improve student performance. The procedure is cyclical in that continuous improvement depends on ongoing feedback of achievement results.

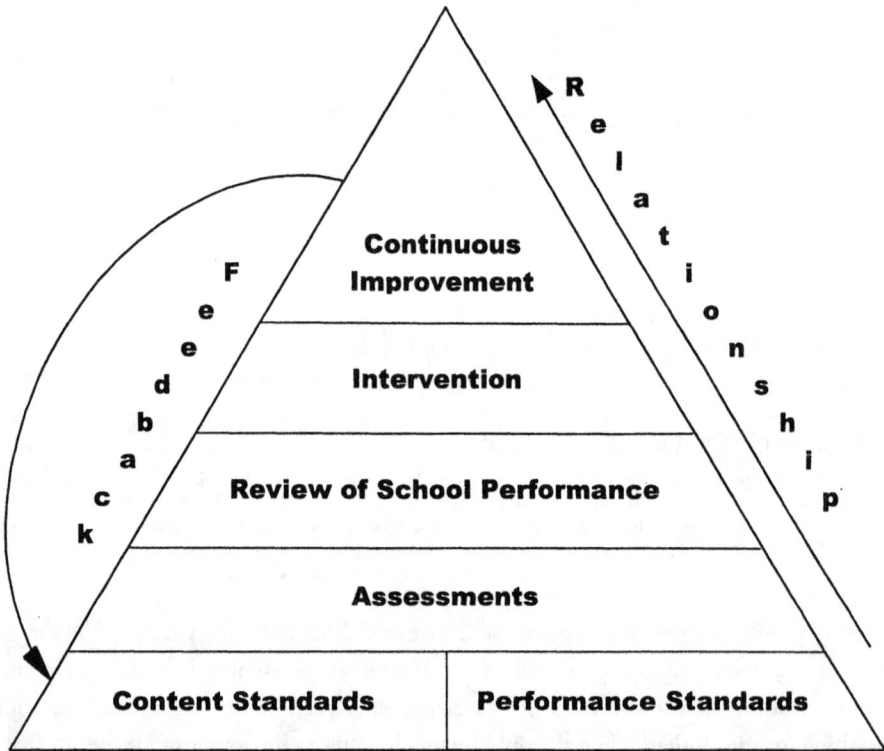

Figure 4.5. Framework for Accounting Systems for Student Achievement
Source: Guth, J.A., Holtzman, D.J., Schneider, S.A., Carlos, L., Smith, J.R. Hayward, G.C., and Calvo, N. (1999). Chapter 10: impact of standards based accountability systems. In evaluation of California's standard based accountability system: final report. Sacramento, CA. California Department of Education. Retrieved from http://www.wested.org/cs/we/view/rs/223.

In turn, each step in the procedure is continuously examined and altered according to achievement data results (see figure 4.5).

The Data Wise Cycle developed by Boudett, City, and Murnane (2005) provides a step-by-step model for initiating and implementing a procedure for using assessment results to improve teaching and student learning. The cycle provides an excellent way for organizing your work and the work of your staff.

The initial procedural steps of *preparing* include organizing for collaborative work, building assessment literacy, and creating an overview of data. Follow-up *inquiry* includes digging into student data, examining instruction, and developing an action plan to implement instructional changes. The final steps include *acting and assessing*: planning to assess progress and recycling the procedure.

Each specific step in the cycle identifies the information of importance for successfully completing the step that follows. For example, after you and the staff have examined current instruction for needed interventions and changes, a follow-up instructional action plan is necessary.

SCHOOL-COMMUNITY PARTNERSHIPS SUPPORT A LEARNING CULTURE

You most likely have read statements in the literature recommending that school leaders engage businesses, families, local and state agencies and organizations, higher education, and other community stakeholders as partners in supporting the development of a learning culture in the school community. Recommendations for collaborating with other individuals and organizations most often lack one important consideration: that's how to do it.

We have never found a school principal that had a magic wand to accomplish their challenging tasks. We hope you agree that collaboration with other community members to identify priority educational goals and discrepancies between present and desired student achievement is highly important. How well do you think your school is doing in this regard?

The terms *collaboratives* and *partnerships* are inextricably related. As noted by the Navy League of the United States (June 2009), "A partnership requires collaboration between two organizations" (p. 4). For our purposes, we use the two terms *collaboratives* and *partnerships* interchangeably.

School leaders frequently express their desire to establish a partnership with a group, company, agency, or organization in the local community. But what do they really mean? Do they actually want one of the organizations to be a true partner of the school? Do they want only to establish a friendly communication with the organization's leaders? Or are they only hoping to gain the cooperation and support of the organization in question for the benefit of the school? In too many instances, all that is done is to advertise the fact that

CHAPTER 4

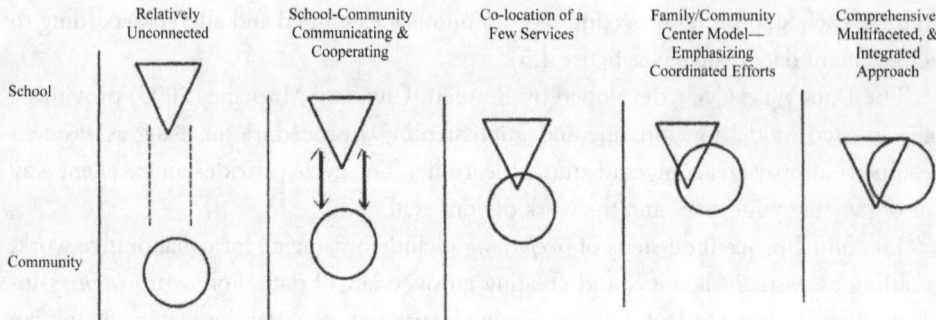

Figure 4.6. Nature and Scope of Collaboration
Source: Used by permission of the Center for Medical Health in Schools, UCLA.

donations given to the educational fund of a school is tax deductible. Doesn't collaboration imply a two-way relationship?

Figure 4.6 illustrates a progression of development concerning school collaboration. Give a moment's thought to where your school would rank in relation to the nature and scope of collaboration. If you are at one of the last two stages, give yourself a pat on the back. If not, give serious consideration to what needs to be done to move your school ahead. This chapter will give you new thoughts regarding the challenges you will face in working toward the development of a school and school-community learning culture.

COLLABORATION AND PARTNERSHIPS: WHAT DO THEY REALLY MEAN?

If one is going to talk about collaboration and partnerships, it seems like a good idea to clarify what you're talking about. You can find a variety of definitions of the term *collaboration* in the literature. Its Latin roots are *com* meaning "together" and *laborare* meaning "labor" or "to work together." In many respects, collaboratives can be either social or academic in nature.

COLLABORATION AND PARTNERSHIPS: WHAT DO THEY MEAN FOR YOU AS PRINCIPAL?

Are you one of the few school principals in the nation that has established formal partnerships with outside organizations? If you have done so and such arrangements have worked wonders for your school and for the organizations, you might want to skip this section.

Yes, school personnel often meet with local community leaders and talk, but purposeful action by a partnership toward a worthwhile result that enhances student achievement doesn't happen that easily. As noted by Adelman and Taylor (July 2006), "Collaboration involves more than simply working together. It is more than a process to enhance cooperation and coordination . . . In the long-run . . . school-community collaboratives must be driven by an enlightened and comprehensive vision about strengthening youngsters, families, schools, and neighborhoods" (p. 39).

It is clear that the implementation of a school and stakeholder collaborative necessitates alterations in leadership, planning, programming, and accountability. True partnerships are about give and take. Are you as principal willing to make such changes?

Learning Snapshot #3—One elementary school demonstrated an academic collaborative when it established a tutoring day for students who needed special help in the academic areas of reading and math. The tutors are employees of a local utilities company. They receive training as tutors and are given materials and directions for instruction in advance by the school staff. The utility company pays the tutors. Tutoring sessions take place once each week for a period of one to two hours.

The result? Most recently, at the end of the semester tutoring period, every student in the tutoring program met the academic benchmark for achievement in each of the two academic areas of reading and math. What benefits might be received by the participating organization? Take a moment to name one or two.

Historically, schools have been quite good at establishing *social collaboratives*. PTA (parent teacher association) is one example. In social collaboratives the purposes of promoting good public relations and informing parents and families about the needs and work of the school are foremost. I think that you would agree that schools have not been as good at establishing *academic collaboratives*.

In academic collaboratives, student learning needs to grow. "School leadership standards specify the need for principals to pay attention to and be involved in the wider community if they wish to make the most of educational opportunities for students" (e-Lead, 2011, p. 1). An example of parental involvement and academic partnerships is described in Learning Snapshot #4.

Learning Snapshot #4—The school principal in one elementary school reported the following collaborative activity. He described his "invite and involve" philosophy by saying that parents of most academically at-risk students were invited to sit in with teachers, the counselor, principal, and other appropriate staff personnel.

Teachers are provided substitutes for one day. The learning discussion centers on the student's achievement status, what the school is doing to help reduce the student's achievement gap, gaining the parents' suggestions relative to the student's needs and interests, providing recommendations for what the home can do to facilitate the student's achievement progress, and what follow-up assessment activities will be administered. The parents gain an understanding of their child's achievement goals and how they can supplement the learning strategies of the school in the home environment.

Adelman and Taylor (2006) believe that "The hallmark of a school-community collaborative is a formal agreement among participants to establish an autonomous structure to accomplish goals that would be difficult to achieve by any of the participants alone" (p. 39). This perspective certainly suggests a relationship that goes beyond meeting and talking. It gives the picture of a more structured arrangement that it has a definite purpose, and all parties are working to achieve important results. Our focus is on collaboratives that center on the improvement of student learning.

Yes, but does sharing leadership with others pay dividends for student learning? According to *Science Daily* (2010), the sharing of leadership with teachers and a wider variety of community members results in higher student achievement. In fact, higher-performing schools commonly ask for more input from community stakeholders.

Community-school proponents express the belief that it is the work of the school to improve the community. They contend that community-school collaborative partnerships improve student learning, promote family engagement, enhance school effectiveness . . . and boost community vitality. London (2011) looks at collaboration as a process of shared decision making; all parties that have an interest in the problem or matter examine their commonalities and differences and work cooperatively to determine a joint plan of action.

The primary objectives of collaboratives are to (1) identify and coordinate resources and services within the school community, (2) strengthen school learning programs, (3) improve family practices, and (4) benefit school partnerships (see figure 4.7).

Clearly the foregoing perspectives of a partnership emphasize (1) implementing a shared decision-making process, (2) using common resources to strengthen school and student learning, (3) enhancing mutual cooperation and coordination, (4) having all parties genuinely interested in the problem or matter in question, and (5) knowing that there is an implication of suggested changes in leadership behaviors. The concept is based on a TEAM approach: **T**ogether, **E**veryone, **A**chieves, **M**ore. Later we will look at the implications of these perspectives for you as the school principal.

Ellis (2011) points out that collaborative processes can be enhanced among teachers by giving them time to meet together for the purpose of instructional improvement. "Given sufficient time and consistent messages about the value of collaboration, teachers learn to trust their colleagues and are more willing to share their best practices and challenges" (p. 3). One way to gain such time together is to arrange scheduling so that grade level teams, subject-matter teams, and other improvement teams share common planning time.

A NOTE ON WHAT COLLABORATION IS NOT

In an attempt to clarify what a concept is, sometimes it helps to think about what it is not. Collaboration is *not* just finding an individual or organization in the community that is willing to give resources to support a need of the school. Rather, collaboration necessitates learning about both parties' interests and needs and how a cooperative effort with the school and community group organization would be mutually beneficial.

Collaboration is *not* just the implementation of a positive public relations program. It is much more than merely working together on some project. It involves more than just engaging the community to gain resources to support the school's program activities or to pass bond issues. It goes much deeper than that.

An effective collaboration requires that you as principal share an important goal such as establishing a school-community learning culture and working cooperatively with stakeholders of the community to achieve it. It means that you must give emphasis to a mutual concern and establish a procedure with the collaborating partner for realizing the desired results. "Collaboratives are about building potent, synergistic, *working relationships,* not simply establishing positive personal connections" (Adelman & Taylor, 2006, p. 41). Collaboratives that are one-way rather that two-way partnerships are likely to be short lived.

Collaboration is *not* limited to school-to-work programs. Some studies point out that " . . . established partnerships between schools and community service providers (e.g., mental health, social services) seem to be limited" (Foley, 2001, p. 10). Dental and vision partnerships, local dance studios, music and art, physical education, the media, police, youth groups, and other fields and agencies are examples whereby collaboratives could be established for the benefit of students in the school as well as organizations in the community.

But how do organizations and businesses benefit by partnering with your school? Local partners have the opportunity to gain knowledge and understanding to better serve the needs of those in the community. Local partners can gain connections with potential future employees. They can add to their organization's purpose by contributing their knowledge and skills to activities that result in improved opportunities for students.

Collaboration is *not* just a one-time effort on your part to clarify the current and future needs of the school and/or to gain community understanding of the state of the school. As noted by Adelman and Taylor (2006), "Building such partnerships calls for an enlightened vision, creative leadership, and new multifaceted roles for professionals who work in schools and communities, as well as for all who are willing to assume leadership" (p. 3).

As you likely have discovered, collaboration places new demands on the already challenged practicing principal. Our intent in this section has been to point out that establishing a school-community learning culture is a challenging, complicated, time consuming, but worthwhile consideration that you should pursue. Why? Because both empirical and research evidence show that it results in improved student achievement and community improvement.

CHAPTER 4

HOW YOU CAN GET STARTED TO BUILD SCHOOL COLLABORATIVES

"Most effective schools find resources by looking in their own backyard—their own community" (Parents Reaching Out, Spring 2009, p. 10). "The 3 top ingredients for effective collaboration would be relationship, relationship, relationship" (McDaniel, Campbell, & Seaburn, 1995, p. 283). Take five minutes to write down several potential community resources that could be beneficial to your school and also to those groups or organizations. Then check your list with the community resource listing set forth in figure 4.7. Does the list suggest other key resources that you may have overlooked?

Directions: Use a blue or black pen to draw lines from Your School to any of the resources (parents and family, other schools, local businesses, etc.) with whom you have present **partnerships**. Then use a red pen to draw lines from Your School to any of the resources that might represent potential partnerships for your school. (Note: Add any other appropriate resources within your school community on the lines at the bottom of the list.)

YOUR SCHOOL •

Parents and Family

Other Schools

Local Businesses

Community Clubs

Universities and Colleges

Health Agencies

Community Leaders

Vocational/Technical Schools

Local Newspapers

Police Department

Child Care Centers

Social Services

Food Services

Art and Music Institutions

Entertainment Groups

_____

_____

Figure 4.7. Potential Resources for Your School Partnerships
Source: Family Connections Series (Spring 2009). Collaborating with the Community: Action Teams for Partnerships (ATP). A Guide for Improving Student Success through Partnerships of Families, Schools and Communities. Albuquerque, N.Mex.: Partners Reaching Out. Coordinator: Jody Fuller.

One strategy that you could implement for identifying potential resources within the community is *community mapping*. You most likely have utilized curriculum mapping to determine what actually is being taught in your math, science, language arts, and other classes. Community mapping serves a similar purpose. This process helps you identify the potential resources that presently exist in the school community. In addition, it helps you to determine those resources that are needed by the school but are not readily available.

Why have we given so much attention to the establishment of collaboratives in this chapter? First of all, recent major students of leadership and student achievement have found that collaboration among the school's stakeholders, from the state and district levels to individual principals, school board members, teachers, and community members correlated with improved student learning (Wahlstrom, Louis, Leithwood, & Anderson, 2010). We believe that educational extensions such as school communities will be among the next important movements in education.

Community financial support for schools through bonding has become contentious. Other efforts for monetary support such as tax credits have been helpful but have fallen far short of raising needed funds. Partnerships and collaboratives have the potential of establishing a base for additional human and monetary resources. Such a potential provides the basis for improving educational opportunities for all students.

SUMMARY

The concept of building a learning culture in the school and school district must include building that culture throughout the entire school community. Partnerships and other collaboratives are of paramount importance in reaching that goal. Empirical evidence suggests that most schools have limited partnerships to social events; positive public relations are the primary goal.

Our perspectives in this chapter go far beyond the PR stage and reach out to the goal of improving student achievement. In order to achieve this purpose, a more structured two-way agreement between the school and community group or agency must be developed. Both the school and the community agency should gain from the partnership.

The concept of what collaboration is not was underscored as well. We submit that collaboration is not a one-time social event or an activity that is designed only to benefit the school. A community learning culture requires continuous relationship as well.

Several practicing school principals presented their behaviors in helping to gain the commitment of the school staff to the leading purpose of student achievement. Behavioral honesty was one trait emphasized by most every principal that we interviewed. Learning-leaders are first to admit it if they do not know the answer to a question posed. But they also are the first to find ways to find that answer and report it back to the party or parties that posed the question.

CHAPTER 4

The importance of encouraging teacher learning-leaders to serve the school and school district was detailed in the chapter. Some teacher learning-leaders aspire to administrative roles in their future careers. Others are able to make significant contributions to the learning culture of the school and school district through service as resource teachers, curriculum development activities, demonstration lessons, mentoring, and other service activities.

Accountability on the part of the school principal, teachers, parents, and others was considered in depth. How you as principal can demonstrate accountability for student achievement was emphasized. You can foster student accountability for their academic achievement by implementing such programs as PRIDE.

The PRIDE model and other suggestions for establishing students' accountability for their own achievement were presented. Accountability is founded on content standards and performance standards. Content standards center on achievement in the academic and behavioral goals of the school. Achievement progress is inextricably tied to agreed-upon standards to guide program provisions and instructional methods. Performance standards center on the performances of students and include the quality of teachers' performances in the classroom. The model follows upward to implementation of various achievement assessments that are utilized to analyze and then determine appropriate instructional interventions for individual students and classroom groups. The capstone of the model is that of continuous academic improvement.

APPLICATION EXERCISES

1. Your school might or might not have one or more viable partnerships with other groups or agencies in the school district. If you have an ongoing partnership at this time, give thought to how well it is functioning. For example, how well is the partnership meeting its intended goals and objectives? In what specific ways is it serving the goals of student achievement for the school?

    How is the partner in the partnership benefiting as well? If the partnership(s) in question is functioning successfully, why not plan to describe this arrangement at some future speaking engagement in the school district, such as a parents' group, civic club, or even the school board. If your present partnership is not functioning effectively, review the partnership section in this chapter and see if there is an idea that you might use to improve the situation.

    If the partnership is exemplary in many ways, find avenues to tell others about its success. Include this topic in your talks with teachers, students, principals, and other school personnel. You might consider offering your services to a civic group such as the Rotary Club. Such clubs have many businesspersons who might decide to visit with you about a partnership with them.

2. Consider the accountability model set forth in figure 4.5. Schedule an achievement improvement session with the faculty. Use the model to examine your school's status relative to the recommended procedures. Such a session can serve to confirm the fact that your school is on the right track and motivate faculty personnel to continue to do their best. Such an exercise will also serve to clarify further achievement goals and objectives.

    In some cases, soft spots in your procedures might be identified. In this case, a focus on their improvement will be beneficial to all concerned.

3. Here's a challenge. Ask each teacher to take a few minutes of class time to gain input from students in the school. For example, you might ask each of them to pose a general question such as, "All of us want our school to be the best. What can we do to make it even better?"

REFERENCES

Adelman, H.S., & Taylor, L. (July 2006). School and community collaboration to promote a safe learning environment. *Journal of the National Association of State School Boards.* The State Education Standard, July 2006.

Atkinson, M., & Sturges, J. (2003). *At the turning point—The young adolescent learner.* Boston, Mass.: Center for Collaborative Education.

Boudett, K.P., City, E.A., & Murnane, R.J. (2005). *Data wise: A step-by-step guide to using assessment results to improve teaching and learning.* Cambridge, Mass.: Harvard Educational Press.

Ellis, T. (December 8, 2011). Role of principal leadership in improving student achievement, Broad goals for school leaders. Reading Topics A-Z, Reading Rockets. From http://www.readingrockets.org/article/25981/.

e-Lead (2011). *Connecting schools, families and communities.* Retrieved November 5, 2011, from http://www.e-lead.org/principles/conections.asp. Washington, D.C.: author.

Foley, R.M. (2001). Professional development needs of secondary school principals of collaborative-based service delivery models. *The High School Journal,* 85(1), pp. 10–23.

Goertz, M.E., & Duffy, M.C. (2001). *Assessments and accountability systems in the 50 states.* CPRE Research Report Series, RR-046. Consortium Policy Research in Education. University of Pennsylvania, Graduate School of Education.

Gregorc, A. (2011). *Mind styles.* Retrieved November 13, 2011 from http://web.cortland.edu/andersmd/learning/Gregorac.htm.

Guth, J.A., Holtzman, D.J., Schneider, S.A., Carlos, L., Smith, J.R., Hayward, G.C., & Calvo, N. (1999). Chapter 3: Conceptual framework. In *Evaluation of California's Standards-Based Accountability System: Final Report.* Sacramento, Calif.: California Department of Education. Retrieved from http://www.wested.org/cs/we/view/223.

Kolb, D. (2011). *Kolb learning styles.* Retrieved on November 14, 2011, from http://www.businessballs.com/kolbearningstyles.htm.

London, S. (2011). *Collaboration and community.* Retrieved in 2011 from http://www.scott london.com/reports/ppcc.html.

McDaniel, S.H., Campbell, T.L., & Seaburn, D.B. (1995). Principles for collaboration on between health and mental health providers in primary care. *Family Systems Medicine,* 13, 283–98.

Mednick, A. (2003). The heart of student learning and leadership: Relationships, respect and responsibility, 3(2), pp. 4–5. Boston, Mass.: Center for Collaborative Education.

Miller, R.T., Murnane, R.J., & Willett, J.B. (August 2007). *Do teacher absences impact student achievement? Longitudinal evidence from one urban school district.* NBER Working Paper Series. Working Paper 13356. Cambridge, Mass.: National Bureau of Economic Research.

Navy League of the United States (June, 2009). A partnership requires collaboration between two organizations. *Guide for Council Partnerships.* Arlington, Va.: author.

Norris School District (2011). *A parent guide to the NWEA assessments.* Retrieved on November 17, 2011, from http://www.norris160.org/resource/lienemannt/a-parent-guide-to-the-nwea-assessment.htm.

Norton, M.S. (2008). *Human resources administration for educational leaders.* Thousand Oaks, Calif.: Sage.

Norton, M.S., Kelly, L.K., & Battle, A.R. (2012). *The principal as student advocate: A guide for doing what's best for all students.* Larchmont, N.Y.: Eye on Education.

Parents Reaching Out (Spring 2009). Family Connections Series. Collaborating with the community: Action teams for partnerships. *A Guide for Improving Student Success through Partnerships of Families, Schools and Communities.* Parents Reaching Out, Albuquerque, N.Mex.

Pitkoff, E. (1993). Teacher absenteeism: What administrators can do. *NASSP Bulletin,* 75(551), 39–45.

Popham, W.J. (Summer 2010). Assessment illiteracy: Professional suicide. *UCEA Review,* 51(2), pp. 1–4.

Science Daily (July 21, 2010). *Educational leadership linked to student achievement in large U.S. Study,* from http://www.sciencedaily.com/releases. 2010/07/100721112222232.htm.

Summers, A., & Raivetz, M. (1982). What helps fourth grade students to read? In *Productivity Assessments in Education,* Anita Summers (Ed.). San Francisco, Calif.: Jossey Bass, Inc.

Wahlstrom, K., Louis, K.S., Leithwood, K., & Anderson, S.E. (July, 2010). *Learning from leadership: Investigating the links to improved student learning.* Center for Applied Research and Educational Improvement/University of Minnesota, Ontario Institute for Studies in Education/University of Toronto.

Ward Traditional School (June 2011). *Ward 2011–2012 parent handbook: Ability, excellence, attitude.* Tempe, Ariz.: author.

Webb, L.D., & Norton, M.S. (2004). *Human resources administration: Personnel issues and needs in education.* Upper Saddle River, N.J.: Merrill, an imprint of Prentice Hall.

White, K. (2011–2012). *Common planning time (CPT) summary.* A form used to summarize the results of achievement team meetings. Fuller Elementary School, Tempe, Ariz.

21st Century Learning (February 17, 2007). *Century learning: Teacher as learner.* Retrieved February 17, 2007, from http://21centurylearning.typepad.com/blog/2007/02/teacher-as-lead.htm.

5

THE PRINCIPAL: A LEARNING-LEADER AT WORK

Our focus in this book has been to provide you, the leader of learning at your school, with the information and tools that promote student achievement as well as to report specific experiences of practicing learning-leaders. We believe the information and tools in this chapter will equip and enable you to maximize your effectiveness as the learning-leader of your school. We began in chapter 1 by suggesting that you complete the Learning-Leader's Traits Assessment (LLTA). Upon reflection, what did you learn about yourself? What personal strengths did you discover? Were there aspects of a learning-leader's style or behaviors that were missing? Did you take action to more effectively incorporate those elements that were missing into your day-to-day activities?

In chapter 2, we offered a number of suggestions on ways for you to prepare, equip, and enable your faculty to become learning-leaders in their own right. We presented the characteristics of a learning-centered school and built a case for becoming a school that is even more learning-centered. The importance of utilizing data to drive decision making was stressed along with the value of collaboration between and among your faculty, your staff, and yourself. In conjunction with those ideas, we urged you to view your school as a learning organization by offering opportunities for learning to every member of your school community.

The foundation for a learning-centered school or organization lies in the culture and climate of the school. We noted the differences between as well as the importance of climate and culture in chapter 3. The core values and beliefs held by your faculty and staff determine the culture of your school, whereas school climate is determined by the interpersonal relations, social interactions, and organizational processes and structures in place at your school. Culture and climate assessment tools were suggested in chapter 3.

Chapter 4 focused on creating a school-community culture that enhances student learning. The importance of teachers as learning-leaders and role models of learning was emphasized along with a number of suggestions relative to how teachers can promote a learning culture in their classrooms. Learning accountability, learning styles, and building school and community partnerships were also addressed as significant components of a learning-centered school.

This chapter recognizes all of the components of a learning-centered school in the everyday lives of building principals. We will delve into the behaviors and practices of exemplary principals who have demonstrated learning-leadership at their schools. The principal's role in the development of curricular and instructional strategies and interventions is addressed. Evidence of the role of the principal as a learning-leader is demonstrated as we present effective principals' interactions with students, faculty, staff, and stakeholders. Finally, we offer suggestions and practical examples on how to sharpen your school's focus on student learning.

THE PRINCIPAL: AN ADVOCATE FOR ALL STUDENTS

The principal who aspires to have a school centered and focused on student learning will first and foremost be an advocate for every student in the school. We agree, however, that you, personally, cannot reach every single student in your school. On the other hand, you will, personally, be able to reach some. We urge you to do just that. As a student advocate, your behaviors, attitudes, and conversation will be student-centered and your decisions will always be in the best interests of students (Norton, Kelly, & Battle, 2012).

As a student advocate, you will convey a clear and concise message to every member of your faculty and staff that every student needs an advocate. No student will *fall through the cracks* at your school. The student who is underachieving, not participating, not engaged, or not responding to ordinary and routine school or classroom activities will be identified. You will empower and enable every member of your faculty and staff to *take those students under their wings* by taking an interest in those students and doing whatever it takes to ensure those students' success. Effective learning-leaders serve as models in this respect.

One principal of a K-6 elementary school related his practice of greeting every student new to his school at the beginning of the school year. Before the week is over, he has visited every classroom and has introduced himself to every new student, has learned the student's name, and greets that student by name every time he sees the student outside the classroom. Another principal who has made a commitment to every student stated that his school will deliver and parents can expect high-quality teaching and high student achievement for every child, every day, every minute.

BEHAVIORS AND PRACTICES OF THE EXEMPLARY PRINCIPAL LEARNING-LEADER

In this chapter, we report a number of conversations that we had with principals of high-achieving schools. In addition, several research studies are noted that support our contention that principals are the driving force behind a school becoming a learning-centered school. Our intent is to share with you the behaviors, strategies, activities, and attitudes of principals of schools focused primarily on student learning.

Four basic areas of principal responsibilities are addressed in this chapter. We begin with your role in the development and implementation of curriculum and instruction on your campus. Inherent in this discussion is your role relative to the degree to which student performance meets or does not meet the standards and benchmarks identified in the curriculum. That includes how you and your teachers utilize the data obtained from both formative and summative assessments.

A second area of focus in this chapter is the manner in which exemplary principals interact with and support students. Of course, principals of K-3 schools will interact with students differently than principals of high schools. However, the important consideration in this chapter is that principals do interact with students and do so effectively. Specific success stories are noteworthy.

As we pointed out in chapter 2, principals equip, empower, and enable teachers and staff to become student learning centered. Practices varied among the many principals we interviewed and the research studies we cite. However, experiences are real and the results are documented. The examples we relate are proven successes.

Focus on Results

Ulrich, Zenger, and Smallwood (1999) assert that the leader who wants to improve his or her organization's performance will "begin with an absolute focus on results" (p. 170). This begs the question, What results do you and your faculty want or expect to see in student performance at your school?

The Principal as a Facilitator

One principal reported that one of her major responsibilities was that of a facilitator. When she meets with teacher leaders, professional learning communities, or teacher teams, facilitating the group discussion very often becomes a significant role. Facilitating the discussion includes observing the behaviors of members of the group and ensuring that each member participates. For example, teachers in a professional learning community are asked to bring in their student artifacts and common assessments. She will ask the teachers to share with her and the community issues that are surfacing and will ask what she can do to assist the teachers in resolving them.

Facilitating the group discussion includes asking the right questions at appropriate times. Teachers are asked what they need in the way of staff development, materials, or resources. Opportunities for teachers to observe other teachers are provided in order for them to see firsthand how certain instructional strategies are delivered as well as to witness their effectiveness. It is not uncommon for the learning-leader to have administrators from other schools at the school to observe the manner in which faculty groups meet and process information.

Facilitating group meetings can be very difficult because one never knows what issue might surface or how the different personalities in the group may react. In addition, one never knows what the "hot buttons" of an issue might be. Nevertheless, it is commonly found that better solutions often result when people from diverse backgrounds with diverse personalities meet and openly discuss issues. Facilitating groups under those conditions can be trying but well worthwhile, and it is an important role for the principal to assume.

Ground Rules for Facilitators

The principal in the above case recognized the importance of her role as a facilitator while at the same time not undermining the role and position of the teacher leader. Facilitating a group without stepping into the role of the team or group leader requires skill, understanding, and sensitivity.

Hargrove (1998) offers successful ground rules for being an effective facilitator of a collaborative group meeting. They include (1) treat everyone as a colleague, (2) speak with good intent (nothing you say is neutral), (3) ask questions from genuine curiosity, not from cynicism, (4) openly disagree with anyone in the group, (5) avoid attributions about other motives, thinking, etc., (6) invent new options that break log-jams, (7) retract proposals until agreement is reached, (8) embrace breakdowns as part of reaching breakthroughs, and (9) respect confidentiality (p. 147).

You and your committees, teams, or communities may want to adopt the foregoing ground rules. Perhaps you will want to modify some of the above, delete some, or even add additional ones. For example, some group members may be offended by sarcasm as well as condescending or arrogant attitudes and behaviors. References to these may be added as additional ground rules. Facilitator/facilitating ground rules are important considerations for yourself and your teacher leaders as you facilitate group meetings. They even may serve as a staff development tool for you to use with your teacher leaders.

CREATING A CLIMATE AND CULTURE FOR LEARNING

We discussed the paramount importance of creating a climate and culture for learning in your school in chapter 3. Creating a culture or atmosphere where students feel loved, respected, and successful includes the administration, faculty, and staff exhibiting those characteristics to the students as well as to themselves.

Transforming your school to one even more focused on learning in every aspect will require exceptional leadership on your part. As Collins (2001) stated after examining eleven businesses with sustained economic performance, the effective leader " . . . catalyzes commitment to and vigorous pursuit of a clear and compelling vision" (p. 20). That vision at your school means all students will learn and succeed. It includes all faculty and staff learning together, supporting others who are learning, serving as role models and mentors for one another.

Bret Tarver School (Phoenix, Arizona) is a K-6 school and is the recipient of the A+ school award in 2007 and the A++ school award in 2011. This award is predicated on the school achieving excellence in a number of areas. The principal reflected that when she and her new faculty opened the school in 2001, they formulated their vision for the school identifying what they envisioned their school becoming. They wanted their students to feel loved, respected, and successful.

They determined that these objectives could be achieved by developing a school atmosphere where students wanted to come to school every day. This was achieved by a balance of high expectations, exemplary teaching, and educational and academic support for each child. Now, ten years later, the principal noted that their vision remains the same. Evidence of the school achieving the vision is demonstrated, as noted above, by their receiving a second A+ award, which turned out to be the A++ award in May 2011.

Leading with Your Heart

During one interview, a principal stated that she was very much a student advocate. Every staff member was expected to be able to describe the things that are important to her as a principal. Over time, the faculty came to realize that the expectations were articulated to and with her faculty. These expectations ultimately led to every student learning. Steps were taken to ensure that all students were successful rather than just some "subpopulations" of students.

The importance of kindness when dealing with adults as well as students was emphasized. Faculty members were informed that every student on their campus is someone's child, and that child is the nearest and dearest person to that parent. Emphasis was placed on why we educators got into the profession of education. When we reflect on those values and beliefs that led us into the profession, we realize that we wanted to do good things for others. It is those values and beliefs that we translate into our vision and is demonstrated in our leadership.

Compassion

Leading with one's heart corresponds with the argument set forth by Berliner and Biddle (1995) that improvement in your school or any school will not fully materialize without compassion on your part as well as on the part of every member of your faculty and staff. They wrote, "Public schools can never be judged successful until they provide equal opportunities for all, and true improvements in public education will not come about unless they are based on compassion" (p. 348). A culture of compassion will play a huge part when determining a course of action for teacher improvement as well as student improvement. Compassion implies caring, and a school focused on student learning will certainly care whether or not students are learning and will do something about it.

Little Things Mean a Lot

Sometimes even the smallest, seemingly insignificant actions of the principal will build a warm and caring climate. For example, one principal wrote that snacks were provided at each staff and professional development meeting. Additionally, snacks are provided at random times throughout the school year. She sends birthday cards to each staff member—certified as well as noncertified. Actions of this nature are infectious and have a carryover effect to students. As the principal demonstrates a caring attitude toward staff members, the evidence shows that a similar caring attitude permeates the entire campus and has a positive effect on all.

Focus on Climate First

One principal was asked the question, What would you do to prepare your faculty to become a learning-centered school? He responded that he would focus on the climate first. In fact, he and his staff have worked on improving school climate over the past two years. He is a firm believer in shared leadership and that shared leadership maximizes student learning. As a staff, they focused first on improving relationships with one another and building trust in the organization.

Once they were satisfied with the progress they made with their faculty and staff, their focus shifted to building more positive relationships with the students. Since their emphasis on improving school climate, they have achieved noticeable positive results in improved student scores on benchmark assessments.

Tarwater Elementary School (Chandler, Arizona) has enjoyed an A+ ranking from the Arizona Education Foundation since 2009. The principal at Tarwater and his staff have made a commitment to create a climate for learning that is apparent when one enters the campus. Along with their commitment to academic excellence and high behavioral standards, an exemplary character development program exists as well. The program is titled Toro Targets and focuses on five target areas: compassion, courage, integrity, respect, and responsibility. These character traits are emphasized in all interpersonal relationships between all members of the Tarwater community.

During our discussion with one principal, the terms she used during the course of our discussion included *kind, caring, concerned, thankful, listening, giving back*, and *working together*. She felt that as these behaviors and concepts prevail on her campus, the teachers and staff members contend that the environment in which they work has become more safe and supportive.

In this type of school climate, teachers are not afraid of failure. Rather, teachers feel more comfortable and will openly deal with sensitive issues. The principal said, "We look out for one another." The school's documented improvement in student learning has resulted in teachers at her school becoming and feeling far more successful. Teachers are held accountable, but it is done with kindness and from a caring perspective.

PROFESSIONAL LEARNING CULTURE

Marshall (2005) contends that teachers and principals need to be skilled in observing classrooms, giving frank and honest feedback, and assessing unit plans, tests, and data on student learning. In this regard, the principal must be the chief learner utilizing study groups, book reviews, peer observations, and lesson videotapes. "The goal is to create a culture in which nondefensive analysis of student learning is the way we do things around here" (p. 734).

A true learning culture is where everyone in the school is trained, skilled, competent, and willing to share his or her expertise in making everyone else around them better at what they do in the school. Professional athletes often will say about a teammate that he or she made me a better player. The goal of the learning-leader in a professional learning culture is that people in the school will say that he or she—you—made them a better teacher or administrator or employee. He or she enabled me to see how important my role was in educating the students in our school and enabled me to be a part of their learning.

Learning Snapshot #1—The event that follows actually occurred during the 2011–2012 school year. The names have been changed to protect the school and the district.

McKenzie High School is a school with a student population of over 1,500 students and serves five bedroom communities in a large metropolitan area. Looking at the

CHAPTER 5

website of McKenzie High School, you will see five words on the first page: *Honor First, Win or Lose.*

Toward the end of the first semester and well into the winter sports schedule, McKenzie High School was stunned by a major catastrophe that caused the principal to seriously reflect on that motto—Honor First, Win or Lose. He learned that a number of student athletes as well as personnel in his own athletic department had not fulfilled all the requirements for eligibility stipulated by the state interscholastic athletic association. Because of these infractions, the athletes were not eligible to participate in both fall and winter sports.

The state interscholastic association is the governing body that oversees all secondary school athletic events in the state. To make matters worse, a number of coaches had not met the association's requirements. The violations were far reaching and affected every fall and winter sport that had just begun.

The principal, Mr. Brown, had a choice. He could ignore the violations and hope that no one outside the school would catch them. That possibility was not that remote in that McKenzie High School was not a major competitor in either fall or winter sports. His other option was to report the violations to the state athletic association, which would mean he would have to declare the athletes ineligible and forfeit every game in which those athletes participated. Fall sports at McKenzie include football, girls' volleyball, swimming, boys' and girls' golf, badminton, and cross-country. Winter sports include boys' and girls' basketball, boys' and girls' soccer, and wrestling.

In early December, Mr. Brown was made aware of the violations. He immediately halted participation of ineligible winter sports student athletes. He informed the athletes and their families of the requirements of the state athletic association. Within forty-eight hours, the school had resolved every violation, which included the athletes turning in the required documents, completing the required medical examinations, and participating in the medical-related online video required by the state athletic association.

Mr. Brown proceeded to order an internal audit of all of the fall sports season that had just been completed. He discovered the problems were systemic. For example, only nine of the school's thirty-seven fall and winter coaches had met all of the state athletic association's mandated requirements. The internal audit revealed a number of violations that resulted in Mr. Brown forfeiting eight wins by the varsity football team and nineteen wins by the girls' volleyball team.

Ultimately, after the violations were reported to and reviewed by the state interscholastic athletic association, the association found 463 violations in fall and winter sports at McKenzie High School, which resulted in the association applying the penalty of the school forfeiting 164 games. The forfeitures included games played in sectional and state tournaments at all team levels in boys' and girls' volleyball, basketball, badminton, cross-country, football, golf, swimming, soccer, and wrestling. The district's review of the matter found that 163 athletes were ineligible to compete or represent the school on its athletic teams in fall and winter sports.

Coaches, too, were found in violation of the state athletic association requirements. The association requires that coaches complete training programs in brain concussion education, fundamentals of coaching, CPR, and first aid. This training is designed to equip coaches with the knowledge and skills to minimize the safety risks to student athletes. A number of coaches were found to not have completed all or part of the required training.

Even though the principal of McKenzie took the initiative to investigate the matter and report the violations to the association, he still had the prerogative of appealing. He chose not to appeal. In this matter, the principal showed exceptionally strong leadership. Once he learned of the violations, he began an investigation, reported the issue to the proper individuals, stated that it was unintentional, and agreed to take full responsibility and suffer the consequences.

LESSONS LEARNED

You may question at this point why an athletic-related incident is included in a discussion of improving student learning. First and foremost, this example underscores the principal's commitment to the motto or theme of the school or athletic department—*Honor First, Win or Lose*. Think about the term *honor*. Pause and reflect on all of the ramifications of honor—what does it mean? What does it imply? What price is paid when honor is compromised?

Second, it underscores the principal's courage in taking the initiative to report the incident to the state athletic association. A third reason for including this incident lies in the commitment he and the school made to the values by which they claim to live. Think about them in this case—*win or lose*. What was the price of forfeiture? How many student athletes were affected by the principal's actions?

Think about the five words in the school's motto—*Honor First, Win or Lose*. Each word in that motto meant something to the principal. When it came time to determine whether or not that motto really meant what he and the school stood for and were committed to, he displayed the fortitude and leadership to take action based entirely on the full meaning of his school's motto.

Now think about *every word* in your mission statement. Does it really reflect why your school exists? Does it define your school's purpose? Do you and your faculty truly understand the meaning of each word or combination of words? Are you committed to the statement—the words? Is it more than just a statement written on some document on display at your school? Discuss it with your faculty and staff. Be sure that it becomes something more than a statement—that it becomes a driving force that guides every decision, action, and behavior.

CHAPTER 5

CURRICULUM AND INSTRUCTION

Curriculum Development Teams

Throughout this book, we have stressed the importance of the learning-leader working with teachers in groups (teams, committees, communities) collaborating to achieve the mission and goals of the school—namely student academic success. Marshall (2005) supports this approach with his statement that "The engine that drives high student achievement is teacher teams working collaboratively toward common curriculum expectations and using interim assessments to continuously improve teaching and attend to students who are not successful" (p. 731).

That says it. The learning-leader of a learning-centered school will stress collaboration between and among teachers and support staff members. Not only will the learning-leader stress collaboration, he or she will support those groups as they collaborate to improve all aspects of their curriculum, their assessment tools, their data collection and analysis processes and techniques, their related intervention strategies, and their professional development.

Marshall (2005) paid particular attention to the concept of teachers working together in teams and suggests a number of steps that address ineffective practices and widening achievement gaps. He suggests that the best way to ensure that teaching is done right the first time is to require teacher teams to develop common unit plans and assessments. The teams begin with the state standards and identify clear learning objectives, decide on the essential ideas and questions, create assessments to measure student learning, create lesson plans, and develop a calendar for instruction. He contends that teams plan better, generate stronger ideas, and provide better support.

Common Interim Assessments

Common interim assessments give teachers valuable insights into what students are learning and not learning. Marshall (2005) states that it is vital that teams " . . . meet after each unit or quarterly assessment to look at the results and collectively answer three questions: What percentage of students scored at the advanced, proficient, basic, or below-basic levels? In which areas did students do best, and where were they confused and unsuccessful? What is our strategy for addressing the weakest areas and helping students who are struggling?" (p. 733). Answering the last question with appropriate interventions ensures that all students will succeed.

In one school, the ninth-grade team, also known as the ninth-grade professional learning community, created ninth-grade pacing guides that led to the development of common assessments. The team developed the assessments to ensure that they were aligned with the common core standards as well as aligned with what the teachers were teaching. The result was that all ninth-grade teachers of the same core subjects used the same common assessments at the same times during the school year.

This activity produced the biggest change in teachers' instructional behaviors. One teacher, a ten-year veteran, told the principal that, prior to this practice, she thought she was a pretty good teacher. Now she feels she is a much better teacher because of the dialogue and collaboration between the teachers in her group.

The practice of developing common assessments and then engaging in dialogue with other teachers after the common assessments have been administered has resulted in teachers coming together and learning from each other. When one teacher obtains better results than another teacher or teachers, they ask what the teacher is doing differently from what they are doing. The dialogue continues with teachers learning from each other. Teachers become better teachers, students become more successful learners, and the overall culture and climate of the school is enhanced. There is now a reason for dialogue between teachers. Before, teachers were in isolation. Now they are working more closely together with encouraging and positive results.

Interaction with and Support of Students

Individuals at all ages, positions, or levels—parents, children, faculty, and administrators—appreciate being recognized for exemplary performance and achievement. This is especially true with students at the elementary and middle school levels. Among the many reward and incentive programs we observed, we couldn't help but note the following at the Justine Spitalny (Glendale, Arizona) School:

Student of the month luncheons (parents encouraged to attend)
Tiger Paws (an incentive program for great citizenship)
Perfect attendance rallies
100 Book Club

Perhaps you are now doing some of the same activities at your school. The important thing is that you and your staff members do something. You may want to involve students in identifying ways in which they would like or appreciate their accomplishments to be recognized. Students often abound with creative ideas on how or what to do in a way that is meaningful to them.

Jewel Boxes

Robinson and Bunstrock (2011) reported students feeling supported and encouraged as the result of one principal's goal to improve the physical appearance and atmosphere of her school. The strategy she employed was to designate areas in the school that she referred to as *jewel boxes*. Students were encouraged to post their best academic work, which enhanced their feelings of success. Think about how this might improve the atmosphere at your school? Students pass by the jewel boxes, see their work posted, and take pride in their accomplishments. It may also serve as an incentive to students who do not have their work posted to take more pride in their work and to work harder.

Teach a Lesson

Every principal has a major field of study. If you are a secondary school principal, think about your major field of study. If you are an elementary or middle school principal, what subject area did you enjoy most? What area seemed to be your teaching strength? When was the last time you were in a classroom and taught a lesson? When was the last time you prepared a lesson plan? If you have been in the principalship for any length of time, have the instructional methodologies changed at all? Is there new technology that teachers use nowadays?

So you want to get closer to your students. You want them to see you as a principal who is not some person stationed up there in the "front office" but rather a person who is out there wanting and helping them to succeed. How about considering becoming a "special sub" by substituting for your teachers one time per teacher per year? In the secondary school, that perhaps would be limited to your major field such as mathematics or science. In the elementary or middle school, the possibilities may extend to all grade levels.

Think about the impact substituting might have on your students. On the one hand, they see you as *the principal* of my school—the ultimate authority figure. You are the one that meets with their parents when there is a problem. You are the one who sends them home as a result of a serious discipline problem.

On the other hand, they may see you as a person who really wants to help them succeed. They see you as a person who wants to see them learn, who wants to help them learn, and who is willing to step in and help them learn. They will go home and excitedly tell their parents that my principal taught my class today. Their summation and message to their parents might very well be, boy, was he or she good. Give it a try.

INTERACTION WITH AND SUPPORT OF FACULTY

Classroom Visitations

A number of principal learning-leaders reported that they conduct regular walk-throughs of classrooms on a daily basis. Informal feedback is provided to teachers on what the teachers did well, as well as suggestions that are prefaced with something like, "You may want to consider . . . ." One principal stated that she is in the classroom on a daily basis and has committed one-third of her work day to being in the classroom.

When asked, What do you consider the two or three most important tasks, strategies, or responsibilities you employ to ensure student learning at your school? one principal responded that she needed to be in the classroom to see what the students and teachers were doing. That included providing prompt and direct feedback to the teachers both formally and informally. Often a positive comment to the teacher at the end of the visitation or shortly thereafter represents just the reinforcement the teacher may need on any given day to encourage that teacher to continue a sound practice.

Classroom visitations are an effective way for the principal to have an effect on teacher instructional performance and increase student learning. Marshall (2005) recommends that principals " . . . give teachers prompt, face-to-face feedback after every classroom visit" (p. 733). Rather than give feedback by e-mails or by leaving notes in the teacher's mailbox, personal feedback is far more effective. He went on to say that "Follow-up talks are most effective when they happen within 24 hours: Better 120 seconds of feedback the same day than a five-page essay delivered a month later" (p. 733).

Learning Snapshot #2—One principal was completing his fifth year at a K-5, inner-city school. When he arrived at the school, 70 percent of the students were on free and reduced lunch and 50 percent were English language learners. The school was one step away from the lowest-tier ranking academically.

The principal's initial steps were to complete classroom observations. He built a framework around what really good teachers do. Good teachers take the responsibility for their students' growth; socioeconomic status, race, gender, family background, and other such variables do not matter.

It is difficult to be a learning-leader when the principal spends most of his or her time dealing with students who are breaking the rules. He empowered teachers to deal with discipline at the school. They were encouraged to make calls directly to parents when student problems arose. Such a practice reduced student discipline referrals to his office from 280 to fewer than fifteen over a five-year time period.

A common theme among principals of learning-centered schools is that they hold high expectations for both teachers and students. Clear goals and targets for achievement are established on the basis of the student's current academic status. When a student is not learning, the situation is examined and needed interventions are implemented. Ensuring student learning is the school's obligation, a moral responsibility.

This principal noted that the learning-leader in contemporary schools assumes a different role today. Fundraising, student discipline, and related "duties" that have taken the principal's time are drastically reduced; principals today have a different skill set. Principals must be data savvy. They need to know when enough data are enough, what data are correct, what data are appropriate, and how to use the data. Using data implies being able to analyze it in such a way as to identify trends, identify groups of students not achieving mastery, determine any implications the data may suggest, and identify the learning needs and issues that must be addressed.

The learning-leader needs to be an incredible listener; what are the teachers saying about what they know and what they do not know? Serving as a mentor, providing advice, lending support, and asking poignant questions all tend to foster a professional learning school community.

CHAPTER 5

One of the most significant steps the learning-leader took to establish a learning culture in the school was to enable each grade level to function as a professional learning community (PLC). Each PLC had a team leader, but each PLC had shared leadership and empowerment for teachers. PLCs perform numerous learning functions. PLC meetings were held to accomplish such tasks as data analysis, resource allocation, intervention strategies, and faculty communication needs. Achievement benchmarks were examined, problem areas were noted, and steps to remedy and/or enlarge certain program activities were determined. Students were not considered the responsibility of any individual; rather all teachers accepted responsibility for those students not learning by taking action to correct it.

The principal noted many other important considerations that he viewed as being of paramount importance for student learning:

1. He expects teachers to do great work. He expects students to be successful.
2. He gives both teachers and students time to meet their goals.
3. Much attention is given to determining why a student or students are not learning.
4. Parents are involved in PLC activities and are immediately contacted when their child needs learning support.
5. The principal viewed himself as a learner just like his teachers; all are in a learning process.
6. The school does things because they make sense, they are researched, they are data based, and they are the right thing to do for students.

Customized Plans of Student Assistance

South Hills (Texas) High School is a high school of approximately 1,400 students and had received an academically unacceptable status rating for many years before the new principal arrived. In order to improve student achievement at her school, one of her first acts was to meet with each academic department. A list of all students taking courses was distributed and " . . . teachers were asked to predict how each student would finish the school year. Teachers were required to develop a customized plan of assistance for every student predicted to fail a course" (Duke & Jacobson, 2011, p. 37). Each student's plan is monitored by an assistant principal to ensure that every student is progressing.

Quarterly Data Talks

One principal found quarterly data talks with teachers to be an effective way to interact with her faculty. The focus of the talks was on student academic gains while at the same time identifying those students who had not met the standards for the course. She and the teachers collaborated on determining the strategies and interventions necessary to best meet the academic needs of those students.

Data Wise

The principal of Tarwater Elementary School and his teacher teams used a data review process called Data Wise. His teams consisted of a teacher representative from each grade level. One area of focus was on mathematics problem solving. The team looked at data objectively and utilized a variety of data points to drive or make changes in instructional strategies and practices. The purpose of this was to provide greater opportunities to improve student academic achievement as well as to create a more data-driven school environment.

In terms of school improvement, it became a process he and the faculty utilized to target areas needing improvement. They looked at short-term, medium-term, and long-term data throughout the school year. Assessments were given multiple times throughout the school year in a variety of ways. For example, medium-term data collection consisted of assessing every student and then evaluating each student's test scores. Trends were identified, including those scores that trended below the expected standard. Instructional strategies and interventions were then identified and implemented with those students whose scores fell below the standard.

Long-term data collection and analysis occurred when the students took the statewide tests near the end of the school year. Those scores were compared with the previous year's scores, and modifications in instruction were made in those areas where the data justified changes.

The principal commented that the process " . . . has made a big impact on me as a principal learner . . . .[I] have been right there in the trenches learning right along with my staff . . . ."

DATA-DRIVEN DECISION MAKING

This phrase is used so often in such a variety of situations it has almost become a trite, throw-away phrase. However, for our purposes in aiding your efforts to become a leader of learning at your school and in transforming your school into a learning-centered school, it is of paramount importance. We cannot overemphasize or stress too much the importance of your using a variety of data when making school-related or instructional-related decisions.

In their study of the best practices of high-performing schools, Angelis & Wilcox (2011) noted that the " . . . more effective schools in our study continually collect and analyze a variety of data—formal and informal. Schools collect data from a variety of sources including daily student interaction, surveys of students, teachers, parents, and community members, and from results of benchmark exams generated by teachers, departments, and the school district" (p. 29).

One principal told us that teachers in her school collaborated in analyzing student achievement data. Based upon their analysis of the data, students not meeting benchmark standards were grouped according to their levels of performance, and interventions were designed and implemented to address their academic needs. She stated that we do whatever it takes to ensure high levels of student achievement.

BRUTAL FACTS

We borrow this concept from Collins (2001) where he cited a number of good to great companies that looked at the brutal facts of reality about their organizations and then made the hard and relevant decisions to make whatever changes were necessary to become great. Looking at the brutal facts of student achievement or the factors that impact student achievement is the first step you must take in order to learn what you and your staff must do to transform your school into a school that is even more learning-centered.

Looking objectively at the brutal facts of student achievement, student performance, and/or student behaviors parallels what the good to great companies did and still do. The brutal facts about student achievement as well as the factors that impact student achievement give you a solid frame of reference from which to make curricular, instructional, and/or operational decisions. For example, the brutal facts of student performance in mathematics disaggregated by gender, grade level, or ethnicity will give you and your teachers an objective basis from which to decide on whether or not changes in instructional methods, materials, or timing should be made.

Learning Snapshot #3—The principal of McClintock High School in Tempe, Arizona, spoke enthusiastically of the "rubber band" concept. The concept served to "stretch" the thinking of faculty personnel about new possibilities for improving present practices applicable to student learning.

The principal cautioned about stretching the rubber band too far too quickly; it could snap back and hurt. The same holds true with new programs, interventions, and strategies presented to the faculty. Both teachers and faculty can stretch. However, one must use caution and avoid stretching them too much too soon.

As McClintock High School moved toward becoming an A+ school, the need for teachers to become proficient in gathering and analyzing achievement data loomed important. She felt strongly that teachers need to be supported in their efforts to become knowledgeable and comfortable in working with data. They were encouraged to gather and analyze data on a daily basis using various methods of assessment. Of primary importance was the necessity to work with teachers in developing curriculum and related formative student data. Emphasis was given to understanding that developing curriculum concurrently with the development of related formative assessments enables teachers to know and understand what content needed to be taught and assessed.

As the learning-leader, the principal was an active participant and the driving force in the entire improvement process. For example, she sought funds for various staff development activities. Such funding was awarded for all teachers of honors classes to become gifted endorsed. The key point is that the principal and the teachers worked cooperatively to plan staff development activities that served to enhance personnel skill levels for instruction. In this instance, the primary focus of the school was that of the common core areas. With teachers becoming more proficient in the common core areas, such training enabled teachers to teach more effectively. Student academic achievement has continued to improve, and the school's goal of becoming an A+ school is a closer reality.

BUILDING TEACHER LEADERS

Building teacher leadership was a common thread among the many principals interviewed for this book. Comments such as " . . . liking lots of leaders . . . " and " . . . my teacher team has led more through this process than I think I have . . . " build capacity in and among the faculty, giving them ownership of the plans and strategies that improve student achievement.

For example, school teams, committees, or professional learning communities may be organized around grade levels, subject areas, or specific areas targeted for school improvement. Teachers in a specific grade level or subject area may see the need, based on the analysis of student performance, to improve student achievement in that subject area. One teacher may be identified to chair the team while other members of the team may be given the responsibility of collecting and analyzing all the student scores on the formative assessments and presenting their findings to the group. Other teachers may be given the responsibility to research additional instructional strategies and present their findings to the group for consideration.

Zig Ziglar (1990) wrote in his famous bestseller, *See You at the Top*, "I believe you can get everything in life you want if you help enough people get what they want" (preface). Think about that statement for a minute and apply it to you and your school. What Ziglar has said is that the more you help teachers become more effective and successful as teachers, the more you will realize your ambitions to create a school where everyone learns. Can you think of a better "top" that you and your staff could reach than to have every person—student and teacher alike—involved in your school realize their goals and objectives, both personally and professionally?

Learning Snapshot #4—One principal had served in the central office as a director of staff development and school improvement. After years in that position, as well as serving as an assistant principal at another school in the same district, she was selected as the principal of a school in the same district where she knew very few staff members. She began her assignment as principal by doing things the way she felt she should do them, which was reflective of her personality and style.

As principals often do during times of self-reflection, she wondered if she was in the right place at the right time. During the five years she has been at the school, she feels that she and her staff have learned together. She feels that she, in her present assignment, is at the right place at the right time.

As she reflected on her experiences as a principal, she believed that when one goes into leadership, one does so because that person is a natural leader or may feel he or she has a calling. She went on to say that during times of her personal reflection, she thought about what was really good for all of her kids and what was really good for our society. Often this became the overriding theme of her thinking. That thinking led her to visualize how she and her school could make that happen and became the focal point of many discussions with her faculty and leadership team.

The principal felt that the learning snapshot for her was learning how to work effectively with a new group of people with whom she did not have those personal relationships already built. Learning to work with them effectively was a true learning experience for her.

ORGANIZING TO IMPROVE STUDENT ACHIEVEMENT

Organizing or reorganizing to improve student achievement suggests a number of options. Does it mean changing the starting and ending times of the school day? Does it mean creating curriculum and instructional blocks where two or more subjects are taught in a larger block of time than single-period subjects? Does it mean revising the registration procedures or altering the steps by which a student is admitted to school? In this section, we focus on the aspect of time as well as the creation of teams of faculty and staff to better serve your students.

Finding Time

Finding time for you and your faculty to meet and discuss student achievement issues is a significant problem. Lezotte and McKee (2004) discuss finding time for school improvement and offer three sources of time for you to consider: " . . . volunteer time, existing time, and creating new time" (p. A-41).

Volunteer time includes time before and after school, lunchtime, weekends, and summer. Finding time for school improvement from existing time includes releasing teachers from regular classroom duty, combining classes, or making special arrangements in the teachers' schedules. Creating new time may include shortening the school day or lengthening the school year in order to provide more teacher-release days for collaboration and/or staff development.

An outstanding example of a principal finding time for his professional learning communities (PLC) to meet is at Hudson (Tempe, Arizona) Elementary School. He provided a release day for each of his teachers on the PLC, and the entire day was used to review standards, review lesson plans, analyze student achievement data, make decisions, and put together units. Federal funds earmarked for staff development were used to hire substitutes.

Creating Faculty Teams

At the outset, we agree with McMackin and Johns (2011) that "Teams are not committees; teams are much more important.... Teams are designed to do the day to day work that is related to student achievement by following prescribed processes and protocols" (p. 46). Schools today utilize a variety of teams that may include school improvement team, school leadership team, grade level team such as sixth-grade team, school profile team, or assign a team to a specific goal.

COMPONENTS OF EFFECTIVE TEAMS

Because we feel strongly that faculty and staff working together in teams affords you and your school the greatest potential for becoming a learning-centered school, it is important for you to have a model to assess your teams' effectiveness. Huszczo (1996) offers the following seven key elements of successful teams:

1. Effective teams have a clear sense of direction.
2. Effective teams have talented members.
3. Effective teams have clear and enticing responsibilities.
4. Effective teams have reasonable and efficient operating procedures.
5. Effective teams have constructive interpersonal relationships.
6. Effective teams have active reinforcement systems.
7. Effective teams have constructive external relationships. (p. 63)

Now let's apply the seven characteristics to your school and take the school improvement team as our example. First, the school improvement team will have a clear sense of direction or purpose. The purpose of the school improvement team in most schools is to oversee and monitor the overall efforts of the school to achieve its mission and goals. The team participates in the analysis of all the data used to describe the school at the time the school improvement process begins. Additionally, the team participates in the development of the school's goals and objectives for the current school year.

Second, the team members are talented, and each member brings a unique set of skills, background, knowledge, and experience to the team. Team members recognize, value, and appreciate the contribution each team member can make. For example, the team may consist of a teacher of mathematics who enjoys working with data. That person may be given the responsibility of verifying the data and assumptions contained in reports from other teams.

CHAPTER 5

Third, each team member has clear and enticing responsibilities. One person may serve as the recorder while another accepts the responsibilities of team leader. One person on the team may be assigned as the liaison to each of the school's subgoal teams. They serve to meet with the goal team and then report back to the school improvement team the progress or issues faced by the goal team.

Fourth, reasonable and efficient operating procedures are established. For example, a regular meeting time and place may be established. The ground rule of one principal was that the meetings will ALWAYS start on time. He rewarded those who reported to the meeting on time. He also ended the meetings on time or as close to the scheduled ending time as possible. Everyone soon learned to be on time to his meetings. Another might be that anyone wanting to put items on the agenda must submit them to the team leader not later than two days prior to the meeting. In that way, every item got on the agenda, the agenda was sent to group members one day in advance, and everyone was prepared at the time of the meeting.

Fifth, effective teams have constructive interpersonal relationships. During team meetings, team members must feel free to disagree, express alternative views or opinions, or challenge assumptions. In the end, team decisions reflect the position of the entire team, and team members present a united front when moving forward with the decision.

Sixth, effective teams have active reinforcement systems. Reward and recognition systems are in place and utilized at appropriate times. For example, suppose one of the school improvement goals was to improve student achievement in mathematics. A team is formed whose purpose is to develop strategies and interventions designed to improve student achievement in math. At the end of the grading period, the students, in fact, demonstrate the desired improvement in mathematics. Ceremonies and activities take place to recognize both the teachers and the students for their achieving the school's goal in mathematics.

Seventh, constructive external relationships are in place as well. The school improvement team has established and maintained positive relationships with all groups, teams, and individuals within the school. Issues and questions are promptly and efficiently addressed. Communication is open, timely, and clear. Team members are available to all members of the faculty and staff and eagerly seek their input on any matter relative to school improvement.

ENSURING EFFICIENT TEAM OPERATIONS

Given the demands placed on teachers' and principals' time in these busy times, we suggest that your teams utilize a form such as that found in figure 5.1 for analyzing team effectiveness. You may want to give the instrument to each of your school teams at the beginning of the school year and ask the teams to use it as a tool to set the bar for team

Directions: Circle the number (1 low performance to 5 high performance) that corresponds most clearly with your perception of your team's operations. It is important that you be honest and frank in your assessment, for it is only from this assessment and your team's efforts that your team will improve.

	ELEMENT	Low				High
1	Clear sense of direction	1	2	3	4	5
2	Talented team members	1	2	3	4	5
3	Clear and enticing team member responsibilities	1	2	3	4	5
4	Reasonable and efficient team operating procedures	1	2	3	4	5
5	Constructive interpersonal relationships	1	2	3	4	5
6	Active reinforcement systems	1	2	3	4	5
7	Constructive external relationships	1	2	3	4	5

Figure 5.1. Measuring Team Effectiveness

effectiveness. Either midway through the school year or at the end of the year, ask each team to do a self-analysis and complete the assessment. Those areas in which the bar was not reached may serve as points for future training and staff development.

PROFESSIONAL LEARNING TEAMS: TIER ONE

Schools focused on student learning are well represented by the Rolling Meadows (Illinois) High School, where the faculty was organized into professional learning teams (McMackin & Johns, 2011). Teams are organized around specific courses and consist of four to seven teachers whose primary responsibility is teaching those courses. Before professional learning teams can function properly, however, the principal must ensure that the faculty and staff members understand exactly what all students must know and be able to do. These are reflected in a standards-based curriculum.

Professional learning teams are responsible for ensuring that all students master the standards set for each course at their respective required benchmark levels. Professional learning team teachers are responsible not only for their own students but for all the students of all the teachers in their respective professional learning teams. Additionally, professional learning teams are responsible for designing uniform summative assessments as well as the formative processes that measure the level of student achievement in all courses. Creating, training, and empowering your professional learning teams underscores the principal's role as an instructional leader.

PROFESSIONAL LEARNING TEAMS: TIERS TWO AND THREE

Earlier in this section, we referenced professional learning teams at the tier one level as reported by McMackin and Johns (2011). The membership of those teams consisted of teachers who had the primary responsibility for teaching the courses represented by the teachers. The purpose of and membership on tiers two and three professional learning teams differ from the tier one teams. The intervention process for tiers two and three is managed by the school's administrative team.

The membership of tiers two and three teams consists of student service personnel, deans, and administrators. The team's primary function is to evaluate why previous interventions failed to enable students to achieve mastery and to design or suggest new interventions that will help students with previous interventions. Forming professional teams composed of faculty and staff outside the classroom expands the school's resources that can be applied to improving student learning.

PROFESSIONAL LEARNING COMMUNITIES

Professional learning communities offer another option to principals who are moving their schools toward becoming more focused on learning. Professional learning communities enable teachers and staff members to engage in collaborative learning. The very nature of the name of the group—*professional learning*—focuses the participants on learning rather than teaching. Participating in a professional learning community enhances a learning culture at the school. Teachers and staff members learn together. Participants hold themselves accountable as they all recognize they are learning new material, new techniques, new strategies. Each is expected to apply in the classroom what he or she has learned.

One principal organized her school into professional learning communities. Professional learning communities are a high priority with this principal. Communities meet on a weekly basis, and time was allocated during the school day for the communities to meet. The communities examined promising practices or new techniques or shared successful ideas or instructional practices that work. The principal often participated in the meetings but always provided whatever support was needed whenever it was needed.

For years, school leadership teams at one high school were organized around the target area goals established by the school to meet the region's accrediting agency standards. Teachers approached the principal and requested that the target-area goals be imbedded in the work that was being done by the school's professional learning communities. This created some concern on the part of the principal. She agreed to move in the direction requested by the teachers but insisted on some measure of accountability.

To ensure accountability, the principal meets at the end of each nine weeks with the school's instructional leaders (department chairs) and reviews student performance (benchmarks) in content areas such as reading and writing. The instructional leaders bring artifacts from their students, and together she and the leaders review them. Teacher feedback to students is recorded with the artifacts and gives the principal additional information relative to the issue of teacher accountability. This practice has raised the level of discussion between and among faculty members as well as the principal and has resulted in positive results in improving student achievement.

Professional learning communities at this school include the freshman English community, the administrative community, and the freshman focus community. All members of the faculty can be members of more than one professional learning community, but each faculty member must select at least one community in his or her specific academic area. Professional learning communities meet every two weeks for two and one-half hours. Teachers also spend time outside the regularly scheduled meetings.

The communities/teams set goals and submit minutes of their meetings to the principal for her review. This practice keeps the principal up-to-date and informed of the communities' accomplishments and progress. We suggest you take time to reflect on this learning procedure and how it might be implemented in your school situation.

BLOCK SCHEDULING

Regan High School (Texas) was a low-performing high school with approximately 1,800 students. The school had been in an improvement status for a number of years and qualified for federally funded tutors. When the new principal arrived, she discovered a number of problem areas that needed her attention. Two of the problem areas were academic content areas in ninth-grade algebra and English. She created a new block schedule that permitted for double-blocking in those two subject areas. The extra time spent in those two block programs enabled struggling students to pass the two required courses (Duke & Jacobson, 2011).

In terms of reorganizing for instruction, one principal commented that his school incorporated an eighty-minute block scheduling program into the school day. Teachers implemented a program of daily interventions within the block that resulted in a paradigm shift for most teachers. However, the result has been a tremendous reduction in the number of students falling far below the state standards requirement and a significant increase in the number of students approaching or meeting the state standards level.

CHAPTER 5

COLLABORATION RESULTS IN IMPROVED STUDENT PERFORMANCE

For eight years, Angelis and Wilcox (2011) studied schools whose students consistently performed above predicted levels to determine what the schools did to beat the odds. One of the findings was that teachers, administrators, and staff collaborate and share responsibility.

At Jefferson Middle School (New York), collaboratively monitoring student progress has been credited for a significant turnaround in student achievement. As Angelis and Wilcox (2011) reported, "Teachers and administrators have embraced data as helping them identify and address problems . . . " (p. 29). Grade level departments at Jefferson set goals for their subject areas and develop action plans aligned with district standards, benchmark student performance, analyze results, and refine curriculum and instructional strategies. Results are discussed within and across grade levels and across schools in the district.

The principal at South Hills High School took specific action to provide the faculty with opportunities for collaboration. She redesigned the daily schedule to provide teachers of the same subject areas with the same planning period. The time is used to " . . . analyze student achievement data, identify students in need of assistance, and develop new approaches to critical content." (Duke & Jacobson, 2011, p. 37).

INTERVENTION PERIODS

As McMackin and Johns (2011) reported, one school, Rolling Meadows High School, created the intervention period to give students an opportunity to go to any teacher for extra help, make up assignments, or get answers to questions. It is designed primarily for students who may have a temporary or short-term problem. Students are permitted to use the period to participate in study groups or to meet and complete group projects.

MENTORING

One of her first actions taken by the principal of South Hills High School, as Duke and Jacobson (2011) reported, was to form a student advisory group to get its input on a number of issues, including asking students why they did not attend after-school tutoring. Students told her they needed a break at the end of the school day. As a result, the principal established the "Monday Madness" program, which consisted of the school offering tutoring classes from 6:30 to 8:30 p.m. on Mondays. In order to attract students, she arranged for pizza to be served.

Duke and Jacobson (2011) reported on the results of the principal's efforts at South Hills, which included a rise in reading scores, science, and mathematics. Following an application of the State of Texas value-added formula to the South Hills test scores, state officials considered the gains to be "heroic."

LENGTHENING THE SCHOOL YEAR

Schools in the Cincinnati Public School system participated in the University of Virginia's School Turnaround Specialist Program. Robinson and Buntrock (2011) identified one of the initiatives implemented by the school system: schools targeted as turnaround schools would begin the school year two weeks early. Principals and teachers in those schools developed individual academic success plans for students using assessment data to address each student's academic needs. The result of this and other initiatives was that the average fourth- to sixth-grade proficiency scores increased by more than 25 percent with thirteen schools showing marked improvement in student achievement.

VERTICAL TEAMS

A number of principals utilize the concept of vertical teams. Teachers meet, work, and dialogue with teachers from the grade level above and the grade level below. Specific areas needing attention ranging from behavioral considerations to low academic performance are discussed. Teachers are made aware of students who struggle in certain areas and the strategies and interventions the "sending" teacher used that helped the students are relayed. Teachers of "receiving" students alert or remind the teachers of the "sending" students of what the students can expect when entering the new class.

Vertical teams also enrich the culture of the school and enhance collaboration. This is another strategy whereby the principal enables and empowers his or her staff to exercise initiative. Vertical teams derive a feeling of independence, that they are in charge of the students they are sending as well as the students they are receiving. Participating in vertical teams enables teachers to work together for a number of years on behalf of the same students. Keeping informed about and supporting students, even though they have moved on to another teacher, is made easier and enlarges the students' support base while at the school.

ENGAGING AND INVOLVING THE SUPPORT STAFF

Everyone Is Part of the Solution

In their study of twenty-six schools in the state of Texas, researchers in the Support for Texas Academic Renewal (STAR) Center at the Charles A. Dana Center at the University of Texas found seven themes of promising practices in those schools (Lein,

Johnson, & Ragland, 1997). One of the themes was, Everyone Is Part of the Solution. Among other findings, they reported that "... it seemed that everyone who might possibly come in contact with a student was a partner in ensuring that student's academic success" (p. 7). They observed that everyone who worked at the schools, attended the schools, or sent children to the schools had a strong sense of ownership in all students' successes.

Job titles at the schools were not as important as the individual's ability or potential to contribute to the child's success. As a result, "... teachers at all grade levels in both regular and special programs, professional support personnel such as nurses and office staff, cafeteria workers, instructional aides, librarians, parent volunteers, part-time personnel, community leaders, and students were often enlisted to be a part of the team that would lead a student to success at school" (Lein, Johnson, & Ragland, 1997, p. 7).

The principal who is a leader of learning will view every person who comes in contact with the school as a potential resource for helping every student learn and succeed at his or her school. As such, the principal will recruit, encourage, enable, engage, and support those individuals as part of his or her team to improve student learning.

Ensuring Efficient Clerical Processes

Duke and Jacobson (2011) noted that one of the first acts of the principal at Reagan High School was to clean up some of the procedural functions of the registration office. She discovered, among other shortcomings, that students were enrolled in classes that did not lead to graduation. She assigned staff members to refine the registration process, monitor each student's credit accumulation, and ensure that every student was taking courses that would lead to graduation.

Student Learning Advocates

Some schools have created the position of student learning advocate. The primary role of the student learning advocate is to act as a student mentor, advocate, and liaison between families and schools. Student learning advocates work in collaboration with members of student support teams, teachers, and administrators. He or she mentors students throughout the school year, placing emphasis on individual and/or small group support, ongoing monitoring of student progress, and helping students make better choices.

School Improvement Teams

Members of the support staff serve on the school improvement team or subteams of the school improvement team. For example, suppose the school wants to reduce the overall absentee rate. Who better to provide data on absentees than a noncertified person who works in the attendance or registration office. That individual has access to the information every day and can readily obtain absentee data when asked. Having that person on the school improvement team broadens the base of the school improvement team and gives the support staff representation on a key decision-making group at the school.

Suppose your school improvement team chooses to improve the appearance of the physical plant. Why not invite a member of your buildings and grounds or custodial and maintenance staff to serve on the team? That individual will certainly be in a position to provide information on where the needs are as well as provide insight on what steps to take to improve the appearance of the campus.

INTERACTION WITH AND SUPPORT OF PARENTS AND OTHER STAKEHOLDERS

Engaging the Community

In their study of forty-three school districts where low-performing schools were turned around academically, Robinson and Buntrock (2011) cite an example of one principal who took unusual steps to engage and involve parents and community stakeholders in her school. To increase community and parental involvement, she made personal visits to community members, made telephone calls to students' homes, and held monthly breakfasts with parents. This and other initiatives such as a more rigorous analysis of student performance data resulted in the school's doubling the number of students who scored at the proficient or advanced level on current formative assessment data.

Parent-Friendly Schools

One principal stated that he wanted his school to be the " . . . centerpiece of community pride . . . ." He wanted it to be a place where parents and community members felt welcome and where parents were proud that their children attended his school. Numerous opportunities were provided for parents to become engaged in their children's education. For example, events such as the Family Fall Festival, Fall Curriculum Night, Family Spring BBQ, the Art Masterpiece Gallery, as well as concerts and other performances throughout the year brought parents to the campus. Parents were told early on after their child was enrolled in the school that being involved in their child's education was nonnegotiable. Parents were viewed as partners with the school in their child's education.

Fresh Start Program

In one school, the principal and the staff observed that making the transition from the eighth grade into high school can be problematic for some incoming freshmen. As a result, the school implemented what they termed the Fresh Start Program. The program was introduced to incoming freshmen at the annual freshman orientation assembly. Parents were encouraged to attend in order to learn more about the school and make their child's transition to the school more successful.

Building Community Relationships

At the beginning of the school year, one school engaged in a unique practice while extending a welcome to its community members. During the summer prior to the opening of school, all four administrators took a mile section around the school and hand-delivered personal invitations to all the local businesses inviting them to the school. At the beginning of the school year, the principal held an open house at the school where the school orchestra played, refreshments were served, and the community members were given the opportunity to meet some of the students and staff members.

The principal wanted to build a positive relationship with the business leaders in the community and get to know them in a positive light. She wanted the business leaders to know that she and her staff were interested in what they needed from the school and its students in the way of job skills, attitudes, and behaviors. She also wanted the community representatives to see her students in a positive light. The result was the development of a very positive relationship between her school and the business community as well as more business representatives and parents agreeing to serve on the school's site council.

School-Business Partnerships

As discussed in chapter 4, partnerships between schools and businesses abound throughout our country. Businesses have partnered with schools in a wide variety of methods such as direct funding, professional development, donation of goods or services, manpower, or tutoring and mentoring. For example, businesses with a strong technical capability such as the computer or information services fields have been willing to offer equipment or specific technical training to office staff as well as teachers. Businesses with large numbers of employees might be able to offer substantial human resources for tutoring and mentoring efforts.

One of the most striking examples of a school-business partnership was where a large hardware and home improvement chain accepted the challenge of totally remodeling a high school's outdated auditorium. The auditorium had never been updated. Prior to the remodeling, the lighting was outdated, carpet was old and torn, the auditorium curtain was torn and ripped, and the entire auditorium was still a "remnant of the sixties." The business engaged in the remodeling project at the beginning of the summer. They provided the manpower, materials, and funding. The principal likened the scene in the auditorium to a little city—scaffolding, personnel, materials, and equipment.

During the course of the remodeling effort, the principal stated she wanted to make the event a learning opportunity for her students. Students in the business department videotaped the work and marketed the project while students in the construction department measured different aspects of the project, determining the amount of paint, carpet, lumber, and other supplies needed and then computed the related costs. Photography students took photos of the project from the beginning of the project throughout to the completion. Culinary students were involved in preparing and serving snacks to the workers.

The ribbon cutting occurred at the beginning of the following school year, attended by students, staff, parents, representatives of the business community, and, of course, representatives from the local home improvement chain that completed the project. It was a delightful event.

When a school, your school, achieves any contribution at any level of any kind from a local business, the bar is raised for every other business in the community. It sets an example for other partnership possibilities in the community. A bond is created between the business and the school. The business benefits as well in that parents, students, faculty, and staff are more inclined to direct their business toward those businesses that partner with the school.

SHARPENING AND SUSTAINING THE SCHOOL'S FOCUS ON BECOMING AN INSTITUTION FOR LEARNING

We believe, as noted in prior occasions in this book, that you are the major torchbearer for student learning in your school. The degree to which you demonstrate a passion for student learning will, in a large measure, determine the degree to which that passion and that torch is picked up by your faculty and staff and carried on. Zig Ziglar (1975) wrote in his bestseller, *See You at the Top*, "Desire is the ingredient that changes the hot water of mediocrity to the steam of outstanding success" (p. 329). We believe, as Ziglar stated, that the intense desire you demonstrate for your students and faculty to succeed will ignite the same fire in everyone in your school.

Product One, ISLLC Standard II (1996), identifies the administrator as an advocate for student learning. As such, one of the benchmarks for the administrator is that he or she " . . . leads by facilitating the development, articulation, implementation and stewardship of a vision of learning that is shared by the school and community."

Sharpening your school's focus entails establishing a clear vision for your school in terms that are understood by your staff, your community, and your stakeholders. Vision statements need not be lengthy, complex, or lofty. One of your most important responsibilities will be to identify what you would like to see your school become (vision) and engage others in the conversation and development of that statement.

CHAPTER 5

It is entirely possible that for you to move your faculty and staff into a learning-centered school will require change in processes, procedures, attitudes, relationships, and behaviors. That can be a monumental challenge for any leader. Weast (2010) states that "In the early stages, visionary leadership will drive change, but to sustain it, you must shift your leadership strategy to incorporate the work of teams. Teams, in turn, work within a culture. The real work of this stage is redesigning systems and structures around key cultural changes" (p. 28).

Sustaining your school's focus—vision—can be achieved through periodic and systematic reminders of your students' successes, instructional successes, curricular successes, and so on. Public recognition of student successes through bulletin boards, parent newsletters, recognition programs, and the like are ways to reinforce your movement toward achieving your vision. Instructional success is directly related to those instructional strategies to which student successes can be attributed. Departmental or grade level meetings where teachers share those instructional strategies are meaningful ways to reinforce teachers' efforts to move students toward mastering the curriculum.

Sustaining your school's focus may also be linked to your objectively assessing reports, data, or information where your school has fallen short in achieving its goals. Your discussion with your faculty, departments, or team leaders may go something like, this is what our data reflect at this point and this is where we want to be. Now, what can we do to move our students or our school from this point to achieving our goal?

Quick and Visible Wins

Robinson and Buntrock (2011) identified a chronically low-performing, high-poverty school in an urban district in the South. The principal decided that it would be important to pursue quick, visible "wins" to motivate her teachers and to signal things were going to be different. Quick and visible wins encourage, motivate, and give teachers confidence that they can make a difference and give students confidence that they can achieve. It has been said that success breeds success. Quick wins represent success.

Kotter (1996) supports wholeheartedly the notion of quick and visible wins. However, he refers to them as short-term wins and has identified three characteristics of short-term wins. A short-term win is first visible—large numbers of individuals can see for themselves whether the result is real or just hype. Secondly, a short-term win is unambiguous—there can be no misunderstanding. Third, a short-term win is clearly related to the change effort.

Now, let's apply his three characteristics to your school. What would be the most visible evidence of a short-term win at your school that you would want to post for all to see? In conjunction with that characteristic, you want to publicize the most unambiguous. Therefore, perhaps you and your faculty might target student absenteeism as a contributing factor to low test scores. Therefore, might you target as one of your potential quick, short-term wins a reduction in the student absentee rate? Perhaps at your school your faculty could administer pre- and post-assessments in a particular subject or grade level. After analyzing the data derived from the pretest, your short-term win would be the percentage of students who achieved mastery after the post-assessment was completed.

The third characteristic, related to the change effort, involves you and your staff celebrating that your school is achieving one of the benchmarks or indicators you identified as a step toward achieving your school's goals or mission. For example, suppose your school's goal this school year is to increase to a specific percent the number of students achieving mastery of the standards in language arts at the end of the year. The targets at the end of each grading period would be displayed in incremental steps so that by the end of the year, the target number was reached. Posting the gains at assessment intervals serves as incentive to keep moving forward.

SCHOOL VISION, MISSION, AND VALUES

As emphasized throughout this book, one of the major challenges facing you as the principal of a learning-centered school is securing and sustaining the commitment of the faculty to the school's mission and goals. One principal maintained the practice of reviewing the mission, vision, and core values in a school-wide meeting at the beginning of every school year. Every staff member—certified and noncertified—participates in the meeting and either makes or renews his or her commitment to the vision.

The mission, vision, and core values are not taken lightly. Rather, they are internalized and become the driving force in the manner in which decisions are made at the school. They also influence the ways all personnel interact with each other and the students at the school.

We cannot overestimate the importance of every faculty and staff person knowing, understanding, internalizing, and committing to the mission of your school. Jones and Kahaner (1995) observed that "A recent study of twenty-five corporate tools such as customer surveys, pay-for-performance, total quality management and reengineering, showed that managers used mission statements more than any other tool . . . When managers were asked to list the tools in which they were 'extremely satisfied,' mission statements had more votes than any other tool" (p. ix).

In their study of twenty-six schools in the state of Texas, Jones and Kahaner (1995) noted that schools did not simply have a mission. Rather, the schools " . . . had the mission of ensuring the academic success of every student. They did not simply have mission statements. Their sense of mission was articulated in every aspect of their planning, organization, and use of resources" (p. 3).

Think about your school's mission statement. Is it just a statement or is it incorporated into your sense of being as a school? You will have no problem sustaining your school's vision and mission when, for example, you plan your next professional development activity or set the agenda for your next faculty meeting and ask the questions, How will this improve student learning at my school? or To what extent does this align with our school's mission?

STAFF INVOLVEMENT IN DEVELOPING THE SCHOOL'S PURPOSE

Involving the entire staff in developing and refining the school's purpose—vision and mission—ensures staff ownership, buy-in, and long-term commitment—sustainability. One principal noted that she and her academic team leader worked with the faculty and staff in small groups and developed the vision for the school. The groups met daily throughout the school year during the teachers' preparation period. Her style was to sit alongside the staff as they worked to develop the school's vision and mission. Her intent was for the vision to emerge from the ground up. She firmly believed that this process ensured buy-in and commitment from her faculty and staff.

TEACHER SELECTION

The strategy of one principal to ensure that faculty were focused on the school being an institution for learning began with the hiring process. She stated that potential new teachers need to know what she expects from them as a member of the faculty. She discusses the culture of the school and shares with the candidate the beliefs and values held by the faculty and staff. High expectations in a cooperative learning environment are stressed at her school and discussed with the candidate. It is much easier to screen out candidates who do not demonstrate an ability or desire to integrate themselves into the school's culture than it is to dismiss the teacher after learning that he or she does not meet the professional standards or expectations of the school.

Answers to questions that focus on student learning during the interview process provide valuable insight into the candidate's focus on learning. Some of the questions reported by principals include the following:

How do you utilize data to improve student achievement in your classroom?
How do you group students to ensure all learners are successful?
How do you differentiate your instruction to best meet the needs of your students?
How do you measure student learning and how frequently do you measure it?
What do you do if you learn that a small group of students has mastered the learning objective while a larger group still needs assistance?
How do you use summative and formative assessment data to drive your instructional planning?
Why did you become a teacher?

Are you willing to do whatever it takes to ensure high levels of student achievement? How do or will you involve parents in their children's education?

PERIODIC REMINDERS

One principal includes his school's goals in every weekly bulletin that is distributed throughout the campus. The goals are posted throughout the campus and appear on the agenda of every meeting. Progress toward achieving the school's goals is publicized and celebrated.

SUMMARY

The overall purpose of this book is to cause you, the principal, to read, stop, and self-reflect on the degree to which there is a school-wide focus on learning, assess where your school is at the moment, and then begin thinking about what you and your staff need to do in order to become the learning-centered school you visualize. We have purposely written this book as a book with ideas and suggestions gleaned from our research but more importantly our discussions with principals of schools that have demonstrated that student learning is paramount in importance.

In this chapter, we focused on the behaviors and actions of principals who have demonstrated that their schools focus on student learning. These principals are leaders of learning. These principals lead their faculties and staff in knowing how well their students are performing academically, socially, and personally. These principals lead their faculties and staff in knowing about the most successful and appropriate learning experiences in which their students can participate that will ensure their students' success.

Throughout this chapter, we have presented specific strategies employed in a variety of schools that have resulted in the academic success of their students. Several overriding themes were stressed. Collaboration and teamwork between teachers are absolutely paramount. Student learning occurs at its optimum level when the principal and the teachers collaboratively analyze student achievement data and design and implement strategies and interventions that will address learning deficiencies in all students.

We cited numerous examples of principals identifying specific groups on their campuses with whom they work that may appear to the reader to overlap. Group terms such as *teams, professional leadership communities, instructional leadership teams,* and others are shared as they were presented to us by the principals. The same holds true relative to our discussion of data. The specific data terms detailed by principals are discussed. Those references to groups and data hopefully will resonate with you and stimulate your utilization of some of the same concepts or terminology or develop ones of your own.

CHAPTER 5

We contend that you, the learning-leader, will create a school culture and climate where faculty and staff feel comfortable in openly sharing and discussing problems, issues, ideas, and suggestions. Finally, you, the learning-leader, must have a vision of what your school not can *but will* become—a place where everyone learns.

APPLICATION EXERCISES

1. Often, mission or vision statements appear like the ones shown below. Mission statements must be meaningful, applicable, understood, and guide decision making. Read each of the statements below and reflect on them for a few minutes. Now, take the second statement and answer the questions that appear below.

Q1. What are the key components of the statement? What words or phrases does the statement contain that drive commitment, decisions, actions, and measurements?
A1. The _____ school strives to foster a . . . "positive environment."

Let's stop there. How would the school define a "positive environment"? What would the visitor see in a "positive environment"? What student, faculty, and staff behaviors would the visitor observe in a "positive environment"? To what extent does a "positive environment" currently exist at the school? Where are the gaps between a "positive environment" and one that is not so positive? What action must you and the faculty and staff take in order to create a more "positive environment" at your school? What indicators will you look for? How will you measure them?
A2. The school strives to foster a . . . "positive, comprehensive academic" environment. Follow the same set or type of questions as you analyze "comprehensive academic."

_____ school is committed to academic excellence. This is accomplished through high expectations, a caring learning environment, consistent discipline, and the partnership among students, staff, and parents. The traditional philosophy is the cornerstone to the success and lifelong learning of our students.

_____ school strives to foster a positive, comprehensive academic and cocurricular environment in which excellence and ethics are the cornerstone of success.

The vision of _____ school is to create an environment that fosters a belief in the importance of lifelong learning. To this end, students, staff, and community will collaborate and communicate on the best means of creating a respectful environment that encourages student achievement.

The mission of _____ school is to provide a safe and positive learning environment, high standards for academic and behavioral excellence, trusting and respectful relationships, and varied learning opportunities.

Figure 5.2.

A3. The school strives to foster a . . . "positive cocurricular" environment. Follow the same type of type and or level of analysis.

A4. " . . . in which excellence . . . . is (are) the cornerstone of success." Conduct the same analysis.

A5. " . . . in which ethics . . . is (are) the cornerstone of success." Conduct the same analysis.

2. With your faculty and staff, conduct the same analysis of each word, phrase, or component within the statement and determine its meaning, the ramifications, and the observable or measurable indicators. This activity becomes a soul-searching activity during which you, your faculty, and staff will determine the degree to which you are willing to make a commitment to the statement. At this point, it becomes more than a statement. It becomes a driving force behind interpersonal relationships and the decisions you make.

	CHARACTERISTIC					
1	The purpose of our group (committee, team, or community) is well known, understood, and is committed to by all members of our group.	1	2	3	4	5
2	An attitude of learning is reflected in group meetings as well as by each member of the group.	1	2	3	4	5
3	Each member of the group contributes to the group discussion openly and honestly.	1	2	3	4	5
4	Each member of the group listens intently in order to fully understand other members of the group.	1	2	3	4	5
5	Our principal facilitates our group's discussions without being overpowering.	1	2	3	4	5
6	Opposing points of view are encouraged.	1	2	3	4	5
7	Decisions in our group are made by consensus and are supported by all group members at the point of implementation.	1	2	3	4	5
8	Group members always discuss matters in terms of "what's best for our students" rather than in terms of winning or losing.	1	2	3	4	5
9	The environment of our group is one of empowering and enabling others to better serve our students.	1	2	3	4	5
10	The faculty and staff at our school openly share ideas with and are openly supportive of others.	1	2	3	4	5

Figure 5.3.

3. The chart below has been adapted from Hargrove's (1998) *Mastering the Art of Creative Collaboration*. Using the chart, either individually or as a group, assess the degree to which your committee, team, community, or school embraces the characteristics of collaboration. A rating of 5 is high, while a rating of 1 is low. Use your or your group's assessments as points of discussion in order ensure a more collaborative group operation.

4. We are sure you have asked yourself time and again, is this the best use of my time? Is what I am doing at the moment in the best interests of the students in my school? Does what you are doing reflect what you truly feel you should do in order to improve student achievement at your school? We have developed the form below identifying some of the key or major activities of the principal. You may want to develop your own form to include the activities you deem most important.

Utilizing the form, keep track of your meetings by placing a simple hash mark in the appropriate column. You may want to record the number of incidents for one day, for certain days of the week such as Tuesday and Thursday or Monday, Wednesday, and Friday, or for the entire week. The important thing is to determine

ACTIVITY	M	T	W	TH	F
Classroom visitations					
Meet with teachers one on one					
Meet with teacher groups (teams, committees, professional learning communities)					
Meet with parents & students re: discipline problems					
Meet with parents & students re: academic problems					
Meet with district or central office personnel					
Meet with your administrative team					
Meet with your leadership team					
Meet with individual students (academic- or behavior-related issues)					
Meet with groups of students (student council, etc.)					
Meet with office personnel					
Meet with custodial and maintenance personnel					
Meet with support personnel (counseling, health)					

Figure 5.4.

where and with whom you are spending your time. Then, you will want to determine if that is how, where, and with whom you really need or want to spend your time to best serve your students and your teachers.

At the end of the time period you select, notice where and how you spent your time. Is that where and with whom you should be spending your time? Are these activities having the greatest impact on student learning at your school? You may even want to "drill down" in some of the areas. For example, suppose you discover that you are spending more time than you realized with certain teacher groups. Evaluate or reflect on the group's agenda. What are you discussing? Why are you meeting? Are the topics discussed in the best interests of students? Are you really looking at the kinds of information or data that will result in improving student learning at your school?

REFERENCES

Angelis, J.I., & Wilcox, K.C. (2011). Poverty, performance, and frog ponds: What best-practice research tells us about their connections. *Kappan*, 93(3), pp. 26–31.

Berliner, D.C., & Biddle, B.J. (1995). *The manufactured crisis: Myths, fraud, and the attack on America's public schools*. Reading, Mass.: Addison-Wesley Publishing Company.

Collins, J. (2001). *Good to great: Why some companies make the leap . . . and others don't*. New York: Harper-Collins.

Duke, D., & Jacobson, M. (2011). Tackling the toughest turnaround—low-performing high schools. *Kappan*, 92(5), pp. 34–38.

Hargrove, R. (1998). *Mastering the art of creative collaboration*. New York: McGraw Hill Business-Week Books.

Huszczo, G.E. (1996). *Tools for team excellence: Getting your team into high gear and keeping it there*. Mountain View, Calif.: Davies-Black Publishing.

Interstate School Leaders Licensure Consortium, Standards for School Leaders (1996) Washington, D.C.: Council of State School Officers.

Jones, P. & Kahaner, L. (1995). *Say it and live it: The 50 corporate mission statements that hit the mark*. New York: Doubleday.

Kotter, J.P. (1996). *Leading change*. Boston, Mass.: Harvard Business School Press.

Lein, L., Johnson, J.F., & Ragland, M. (1997). *Promising practices. Successful Texas schoolwide programs: Research study results*. The Charles A. Dana Center. The University of Texas at Austin.

Lezotte, L.W., & McKee, K.M. (2004). *Implementation guide: Assembly required: A continuous school improvement system*. Okemos, Mich.: Effective Schools Products, Ltd.

Marshall, K. (2005). It's time to rethink teacher supervision and evaluation. *Phi Delta Kappan*, 86(10), pp. 727–35.

McMackin, H., & Johns, C. (2011). Systems change: Response to intervention in secondary schools. *Principal Leadership*, 12(3), pp. 44–48.

Norton, M.S., Kelly, L.K., & Battle, A.R. (2012). *The principal as student advocate: A Guide for doing what's best for all students*. Larchmont, N.Y.: Eye on Education.

CHAPTER 5

Robinson, W.S., & Bunstrock, L.M. (2011). Turnaround necessities. *The School Administrator*, 68(3), pp. 22–27.

Ulrich, D., Zenger, J., & Smallwood, N. (1999). *Results-based leadership: How leaders build the business and improve the bottom line.* Boston, Mass.: Harvard Business School Press.

Weast, J.D. (2010). Deliberate excellence: Five stages to school system maturity leading to college-ready graduates. *The School Administrator*, 67(6), pp. 25–29.

Ziglar, Z. (1975). *See you at the top.* Gretna, La.: Pelican Publishing Company.

About the Authors

Dr. M. Scott Norton has served in teaching and administrative positions in the public schools and in institutions of higher education. He served as a teacher and as a coordinator of curriculum in the Lincoln Public Schools in Nebraska and as an assistant superintendent in charge of instruction and superintendent of schools in Kansas. His experience in higher education includes the positions of professor and vicechairman of the Department of Educational Administration and Supervision at the University of Nebraska-Lincoln and as chairman of the Department of Educational Administration and Policy Studies, Arizona State University.

He has held state and national positions as the executive director of the Nebraska Association of School Administrators and president of the Arizona School Administrators Higher Education Division. His association with the University Council of Educational Administration (UCEA) included roles as treasurer and staff associate. He was the regional representative for the National Association of Secondary School Principals (NASSP).

One of Dr. Norton's most recent publications, *The Principal as Student Advocate: A Guide for Doing What's Best for All Students* (with Kelly & Battle), was published by Eye on Education. Other publications include books in the areas of human resources administration, the school superintendency, executive leadership, managing money and people, and mathematics.

The American School Personnel Administrators Association, the University Council for Educational Administrators, Inc., the Arizona School Administrators, Inc., and the Arizona Educational Research Organization are among the national and state associations

ABOUT THE AUTHORS

that have recognized Dr. Norton for his distinguished service to the field of educational administration and supervision.

Dr. Larry K. Kelly has been a lifelong contributor to education nationally and internationally. He has served as a teacher and as an administrator in the public school sector and as an adjunct professor in higher education. Dr. Kelly's public school service includes roles as a classroom teacher, assistant principal, school principal, assistant superintendent, and director of curriculum. In addition, he served as the director of staff development and directed the Arizona Administrative Assessment Center sponsored by the National Association of School Principals (NASSP).

He served as an adjunct professor at Arizona State University for several years, where he taught courses in competency-based administration. He served as an NCA/CITA Accreditation team member and chair in Arizona as well as internationally for over thirty years. His services as a hearing officer for student and teacher review cases are used widely in the Phoenix, Arizona, area.

In 2006, Dr. Kelly received UCEA's Excellence in Educational Leadership Award, and in 2007 he was inducted into the Mary Fulton College of Education Hall of Fame at Arizona State University for his professional educational contributions to the State of Arizona.

Dr. Kelly's professional publications include the coauthorship of *The Principal as Student Advocate: A Guide to Doing What's Best for All Students* and *Resource Allocation: Managing Money and People,* both published by Eye on Education. Other publications include works in the area of leadership for staff development and student self-scheduling.

Dr. Kelly served in leadership positions in Arizona Association for Supervision and Curriculum Development and Phi Delta Kappa.

www.ingramcontent.com/pod-product-compliance
Lightning Source LLC
Chambersburg PA
CBHW080938300426
44115CB00017B/2872